Conversation
Starters

Conversation Starters

1,000 Creative Ways to Talk to Anyone about Anything

Kim Chamberlain

Skyhorse Publishing

Skyhorse Publishing books may be purchased in bulk at special discounts for sales promotion, corporate gifts, fund-raising, or educational purposes. Special editions can also be created to specifications. For details, contact the Special Sales Department, Skyhorse Publishing, 307 West 36th Street, 11th Floor, New York, NY 10018 or info@skyhorsepublishing.com.

Skyhorse® and Skyhorse Publishing® are registered trademarks of Skyhorse Publishing, Inc.®, a Delaware corporation.

Visit our website at www.skyhorsepublishing.com.

10 9 8 7 6 5 4 3 2 1

Library of Congress Cataloging-in-Publication Data is available on file.

Cover design by Eve Siegel

Print ISBN: 978-1-62914-535-8
Ebook ISBN: 978-1-62914-908-0

Printed in the United States of America

CONTENTS

INTRODUCTION

Welcome to *Conversation Starters*, a book for creative people who would like to have conversations ranging from the traditional, the interesting and the unique, through to the quirky.

Why a conversation starters book that includes quirky questions for creative people?

Conversation has many aspects and is often made up of layers, a bit like an onion. On the face of it, it may appear that we are having a simple conversation, but peel away a layer or two and you may find other issues beneath the surface.

For example, in the previous conversation starters book, *Woman to Woman*, the underlying purpose of the conversation starters is twofold: to help people work on developing their conversation skills and to help with building relationships through conversation.

The underlying aims of this book are to provide the opportunity for you to:

- Develop your thinking skills: stimulate your brain and keep your mind sharp and flexible; try new or different ways of thinking; mentally grapple with new concepts; learn from others.

- Develop creativity: take your brain to a space where the creative juices can flow.
- Enhance problem-solving skills: develop new and unusual ways of looking at issues; try out different strategies; gain a new angle on logic and reasoning.
- Develop conversation skills: work on your speaking skills and techniques.
- Have fun!

A very easy book to dip into, *Conversation Starters* is suitable for people of all ages and contains conversation-starter topics that are thought-provoking, intellectual, thorny, unusual, lighthearted, and amusing.

Being creative allows you to produce new ideas and new thoughts. The conversation starters provide the opportunity for new ways of looking at issues; a chance to be listened to; a chance to work out what your thoughts are on a topic; an opportunity to discuss serious issues; a way to connect with others; an avenue to learn new things; a way to find out more about other people; as well as a chance for fun and laughter. They may allow you to open up new areas of discussion, perhaps discuss a subject you haven't talked—or even thought—about before.

Even if you wouldn't describe yourself as creative, using the book will give you the chance to think in creative ways.

The topics offer a great way to be able to move away from traditional conversation themes, along with the opportunity to develop your speaking and communication skills.

USING THE BOOK

One of the benefits of this book is that you can use it for as long or short a period as you like, either in one-on-one situations or in a group. You can simply dip into it when you are with others and would like to have a quick conversation; you can use it for more in-depth conversations; you can use it for icebreakers; and you can create the right environment and use it as a way to build deeper connections or mentally tackle an issue with other people. You can even use the starters on your own to learn how to formulate responses, develop your creative-thinking and problem-solving skills, and work on your conversation skills.

In addition to the 1,000 conversation starters, the book includes tips, techniques, and quotes relating to four aspects of quirky conversation starters: Creativity, Conversation, Thinking in New and Different Ways, and Problem Solving.

1. How the book is organized

Developing conversation skills

This section contains a simple overview as to what conversation is about, the fundamental principles of conversing with others, and several aspects you can work on to develop your speaking skills. It is complemented by the quotes about conversation included throughout the book.

Developing creative thinking and problem-solving skills

This section provides you with suggestions you can use when working through the book, or to use in general life. It includes a range of techniques and strategies to develop your creative thinking and problem-solving skills.

Conversation starters

The starters are grouped into one hundred different topic sections, each containing ten questions or starters. The topic sections are in alphabetical order starting with Adverts, wending their way through many and wide-ranging topics, and ending with Your Call!

The starters fall into many different types of categories, including ones that pose hypothetical questions ("If you had to classify all the books in a library into just three main categories, what categories would you choose?"); ones that put forward new concepts and ask for your views on them ("What could be the benefits of combining a dog grooming parlor and a vegetarian café?"); different ways of using traditional items ("What else could you use underpants for?"); topics that you wouldn't generally address in regular conversation ("What would you ask Billy the Kid if you were to interview him?"); plus an opportunity to be an advice columnist who gives quirky but useful advice.

At the end of the book there is space for you to make a note of any of your favorite starters or to compile some of your own.

Quotes

Quotes can provide interesting insights into topics, and different angles to view issues from. They can help develop your thinking about an issue and perhaps give you an outlook you hadn't considered before.

There are dozens of quotes on different topics by a wide variety of people included among the conversation starters. They fall into four categories:

- Those relating to conversation skills (CO)
- Those relating to creativity (CR)
- Those relating to thinking differently (TD)
- Those relating to problem solving (PS)

The letters (CO), (CR), (TD), or (PS) will be found in front of each quote.

2. How to deal with quirky questions and conversation starters

Create a safe environment

Make it safe

If people are going to move away from conventional ways of looking at things, and talk about and share fresh and different ways of thinking and problem solving, it's important to create a safe environment they can do this in. It is not uncommon for people to have experienced some form of ridicule or punishment in the past if they have made a mistake or done something unconventional, so people will be reticent to open up if they fear their views will not be appreciated.

Establish a framework of mutual trust so that people can:

- Say exactly what they want to say without fear of derision or judgment, especially if you're in a group that includes someone with a dominant personality.

- Take risks.
- Explore new ideas and ways of thinking.
- Bring out all of their creative aspects.
- Try out and develop their ability for creative thinking.

Show respect

Being respectful of other people and their contributions, especially when you may not understand or agree with what they say, is vitally important to get the best out of them and the conversation—and the best out of this book.

Choose the tone

Are your conversations going to be simply for fun? Are they going to be used to tackle current issues you are dealing with? Is it a situation where people can step outside of their comfort zone and try adopting a different way of thinking from what they normally do?

As long as all people are on the same page when it comes to the tone of the conversations, you should be OK.

Understand and be understood

Depending on how people approach the questions and conversation starters, there may be some interesting responses. Here are a few thoughts to consider:

- Creative thinking may not be the norm for some people. They may feel uncomfortable and want to stick to more traditional ways of thinking.
- Some people may surprise themselves and come up with thoughts they had no idea they had.
- Issues in life are often like beach balls—several people may look at the same thing yet see something different. One person may see blue and white stripes, another may see red and green stripes, and another

may see yellow and orange stripes, even though they are all looking at the same beach ball. Another person's view may not be the way you see the situation, and you may not understand their view, but it may be equally as valid as your own.

- Some people really enjoy off-the-wall thinking and will encourage it. However, other people don't enjoy off-the-wall thinking and won't encourage it.
- Some people will totally relate to another's off-the-wall thinking.
- Try being completely honest when it's your turn, without a care as to what people think, while still speaking with respect.
- Really listen. Sometimes you will pick up a feeling from the other person that a lot more could come out if encouraged.
- Help others reach their most creative level; help them to bring out what doesn't normally come out by encouraging them to follow new lines of creative thought.
- Consider this concept: "My knowledge and life experiences have led me to think the complete opposite view, but I'm interested in learning the reasoning behind what you think."
- Creative people often don't think—or speak—in a straight line. The conversation may go off on many tangents.
- Creative people can become very attached to their ideas and may be offended if others don't see the benefits.
- Creative people may focus on a way to deal with the issue without consideration to the feasibility or workability of their idea, so they may not produce a workable solution or ideas that make sense when put together.

- Creative people may come up with a solution that isn't easy to integrate into "the system."
- Creative people may produce some inventive solutions that bring more benefits than could have been imagined.

Gain the benefits

Starters allowing for creative thinking bring many benefits. For example, you can:

- Use more of your brain. Most of the time in conventional settings we don't use our brain to its full capacity because society's norms have already made most decisions for us. Here, however, with the right environment, you have the chance to stretch your brain beyond those boundaries and use it to its full extent. Don't waste this opportunity!
- Allow for risk-taking but keep it focused when, for example, wanting to reach a conclusion.
- Have the chance to paint a more fleshed-out picture of yourself. Let people see your creativity, interesting thought processes, and sense of humor.

DEVELOPING CONVERSATION SKILLS

What's conversation all about?

Think of a time when you have had a truly fulfilling conversation, and the range of emotions and perhaps inspiration with which it left you, and you will be able to appreciate how conversations can add a powerful richness to our lives.

It's useful, therefore, to be aware of some of the factors that can enhance or diminish a conversation and some of the ways we can work on fine-tuning our conversation skills.

Conversation, as with most aspects of life, is multifaceted. Many factors are at play, similar to the working components of a car engine, so many things need to be working in harmony for the conversation to be "right." For example:

- Do we know how to ask good questions?
- Are we staying on topic or are we rambling off on tangents?
- Do we know the point we are trying to make?
- Do we get to the point?
- Are we judgmental?

- Do we use an appropriate level of language for the people we are talking to?
- Do we speak with confidence?
- Do we mumble?
- Do we ask too many questions or not enough questions?
- Do we speak with respect?
- Do we talk too loudly, too much, or not enough?
- Do we make eye contact?
- Do we smile?
- Do we swear too much?
- Do we interrupt?
- Do we constantly disagree?
- Do we let others take turns?

In this book we will take a summarized look at conversation—a brief overview of what conversation is and the skills that effective communicators have learned—resting assured that we can still have some great conversations even if we don't get all the component parts "right."

1. Fundamental principles

Conversation is essentially comprised of two main aspects:

- Giving information
- Building interpersonal relationships

Some conversations may be focused on the information-giving aspect; some may be focused on the relationship-building aspect; while a large proportion of conversations have an element of both in them.

Skilled communicators understand that forming a connection and engaging with others is especially important, and that effective communication is often not just the giving of information but an exchange—a dialogue, not co-existing monologues—where all parties are included, involved, and energized by the connection.

Great communicators have acquired a range of fundamental skills that result in effective conversation:

a) Connection

Forming a connection is at the heart of a great conversation. In general, it can make the giving of information easier, more enjoyable, and more effective if you can form a level of rapport with the other person. This is especially true for people whose personality style is heavily weighted toward the need to feel connected to others.

When it comes to the building of relationships, if we were to place people on a continuum, with effective communicators at one end and less effective communicators at the other, one aspect we would notice is that those at the effective end tend to focus on other people and meeting their communication needs. Those at the "less effective" end, on the other hand, tend to focus on themselves and on meeting only their own needs. Effective communicators generally focus on the "you" and "we" aspects of interaction, while the less effective communicators focus on the "I" and "me" aspects.

b) Respect

Great communicators show respect for others' needs. They know how to draw people into the conversation and make them feel valued. They recognize that people do not like to be ignored, excluded, or have their viewpoints disregarded. They enhance and build on what others say, not overturn it. They create rapport by showing respect for another person's views, whether they agree with them or not.

Great communicators don't have an issue with whether or not to express disagreement; they understand that it isn't necessary to give the impression of agreeing if you don't, as long as you treat the person and their viewpoint with respect. Disagreement doesn't have to lead to ill feelings; having a difference of opinion that is dealt with in a considerate manner can lead to an openness of thinking and can spice up the conversation.

In situations where there are differing viewpoints, a useful approach is to start off by highlighting the areas you agree on. This will make the other person less defensive and will make your points seem more in keeping with their way of thinking. You then have a greater chance of both of your viewpoints being considered.

If there are situations where you find giving a respectful response difficult, one strategy is to use the technique of "acting as if." Think of a person who will typically give a respectful reply, and act as if you were them. This is an easy way to "borrow" a skill you have yet to acquire. Another strategy is to take the advice of Judith Martin, an etiquette expert who says "If you can't be kind, at least be vague."

Respectful communicators aim to be polite, aim to avoid taking too much of the speaking time, and aim to be genuinely interested in others. In general, reasonable people will reciprocate and will also treat the other person with respect.

c) Turn-taking

Writer Jarod Kintz said, "We talked for four hours. Well, I talked for four, and she listened for two."

Another way to show respect for others is to show consideration for the concept of turn-taking. Great conversationalists understand that people don't have to speak for equal amounts of time, but that all people need the chance and space in the conversation to contribute should they wish. They also understand that if there are people who take over a conversation, it will reduce the feelings of connectedness and inclusion and will result in less effective conversation.

d) The flow of conversation

Underpinning the issue of turn-taking is an understanding of the way that successful conversation flows.

Having a conversation is a bit like playing tennis. If one person serves all the balls and the other returns none, it's not a satisfactory exercise and probably wouldn't be classed as a game of tennis. Similarly, if players hit balls that are short of the mark, it's hard for the other person to return them and so the game becomes very stilted.

And so it is with conversation. If one person does all the talking and the other does all the listening, it would be classed more as a monologue than a dialogue. Similarly, if people are unsure of the kinds of techniques to use to keep an interaction flowing, the conversation becomes very stilted.

There are two main ways you can, metaphorically speaking, hit the tennis ball so that the other person can return it and keep the game flowing.

Let's look at this from a conversation point of view: The first way is to ask open questions or say something that lets the other person know it's their turn to speak and that you are interested in what they are going to say. Asking a closed question such as, "Did you enjoy the party?" is more likely to elicit a "yes" or "no" response and is akin to hitting the tennis ball into the net, whereas asking an open question such as, "So what happened at the party?" will usually produce a longer response. This, in effect, is hitting the tennis ball to a position where the other person can easily return it.

The second way is to contribute something to the conversation that encourages the other person to also contribute, without being specifically asked a question. For example, you might share a story or anecdote, leaving the way for the other person to also share an anecdote. If you know they are interested in conservation, you might talk about how you helped out at a community conservation over the past weekend. Or you might talk about something you know they have an interest in, giving them the opportunity to ask questions. If you know they like a particular author, you may say "Someone bought me the latest novel by Joe Bloggs." Or—when you know them well enough—you might share something personal with them, knowing that they can talk it through with you or share something personal from their own life. For example, you could share the concerns you have about your child who is worried about starting a new school.

If you keep in mind that the overall aim is to enable the flow of conversation, you will begin to use and master these two techniques.

e) Listening

Skilled communicators have invested time honing their listening skills, understanding that it pays many dividends as they go through life.

They know that being listened to is a universal desire and have acquired the skill of being able to listen—really listen—to another person. They understand that listening occurs not just with the ears but also with body language, eyes, thoughts, and heart.

They know that to be a great listener, it's important to:

- Listen more than you speak. In the words of Epictetus, Greek sage and Stoic philosopher, "We have two ears and one mouth so that we can listen twice as much as we speak."

  Although we are taught to read, write, and speak, we are rarely taught to listen, and as a consequence we have less chance to hone our skills and may develop ineffective listening skills over the years. We may therefore think that the aim of listening is to be able to speak and put our point of view across, when in fact the aim of listening is to be able to learn, understand, and then contribute effectively.

  People crave being understood. They also crave being listened to. There is a huge need to bond, and conversation fulfills a fundamental human need to connect. Unfortunately, as a result of social media, digital communication, and the more insular lifestyle of today, people now have less face-to-face communication.

  In addition, while people may have regular conversations, they may not always have the opportunity to speak with people who share the same interests. My brother, at age eight, started following a football team that wasn't based near his hometown. Over the years, he didn't mix with anyone who supported the same team, nor was the Internet available then to connect with others online. At the age of thirty-six he came across someone standing next to him in a bar who also supported the same team. In his words, "Twenty-eight years of football came tumbling out and the poor guy had to listen to me for hours." Fortunately the man was a good listener!

Sometimes the need to be listened to is so great that people regard conversation as a competition to see who can get the most air time. However, the most effective communication happens when we work together and adopt an attitude of give and take. This will involve some sacrificing of attention on ourselves for the greater good of all.

• Be a You-Listener rather than an a I-Listener.

When it comes to the giving and taking of attention, effective communicators aim to give attention to others rather than seek as much attention as possible for themselves. This is the concept of You-Listening vs. I-Listening. You-Listeners focus on listening to the other person, while I-Listeners aim to swing the conversation back to themselves.

For example:

Person A: I've just bought a bread maker.

You-Listener: Oh, that's interesting, what do you think of it?

vs.

Person A: I've just bought a bread maker.

I-Listener: Oh, I bought one of those a few years ago; they're OK if you have the time to spend buying the ingredients and making the bread. Personally I prefer ...

Sometimes it may seem that a You-Listener is an I-Listener, but if you wait a while you will find that they are fundamentally interested in the other person:

Person A: I've just bought a bread maker.

You-Listener: Oh, I bought one of those a few years ago; still haven't worked out how to use it! Tell me what you think of it.

It's OK to do some I-Listening as long as you avoid taking the conversation away from the other person.

I-Listeners can also take the conversation away from the other person by failing to give You-Listening responses. These are responses such as minimal encouragers, like nodding or saying such things as "Mhmmm," "Yes," and "Oh wow!," and support questions such as "So what did you do?" and "Did he agree to it?" If I-Listeners show no level of interest, the other person will stop talking and the I-Listener can command attention again.

- Be as open-minded and nonjudgmental as you can when listening to others with different views. Ideally, let the person finish what they are saying while you spend the time listening in order to understand.

- Understand the difference between hearing and listening and the ensuing benefits. Hearing is passive, while listening is active. Listening means you are seeking to understand the other person's message.

We can learn a lot when we listen—really listen—with the aim of improving communication. We not only learn what the other person is saying, but we also acquire knowledge and skills such as effective and less effective ways to interact, how to ask different types of questions, aspects of patience, ways of responding to challenging questions, and much more.

f) Prepare in advance

Skilled conversationalists work on improving their skills in their own time. One of the ways to do this is to prepare in advance of meeting up with others.

- For example, think about the person(s) you are meeting with. What did you talk about last time? What questions can you ask following up on the conversation you had? What issues were current in their life? What events were going to happen?
- You could find out about things they are interested in and have some conversation starters or conversational material tucked up your sleeve.
- Think through stories or anecdotes you could relate, including humorous ones. People love humor!
- If you are meeting with people you don't know, think of some general topics you could cover.
- If you know people only slightly, think through what you do know about them and formulate some questions along those lines.
- If you feel there may be antagonism during an interaction, think through the kinds of issues that push your buttons. Work out why this happens and devise a way to cope with it, so that you can have a respectful and effective conversation.

g) Conversation Don'ts

There are many things we should do in a conversation, and there are many things we shouldn't do. The Conversation Don'ts include:

- Don't dominate the conversation. The concept of give and take needs to come into play.
- Don't avoid contributing. Most people like to feel a connection with others, and for this to happen you need to contribute, even just a little at first if you are

shy. Start by asking some simple questions. Keep in mind the metaphor of playing tennis.

- Don't ask too many questions so that it seems like an interrogation.
- Don't bring up contentious issues at the beginning of a conversation. Get the lay of the land first.
- Don't leave people feeling negative after an interaction with you. After every interaction, people generally feel in a positive, neutral, or negative state. Aim to leave people feeling at least neutral and, ideally, positive.
- Don't use negative words, facial expressions, or tones of voice. Don't moan and complain or be patronising.
- Don't keep interrupting. It can make people shut down and will have a negative impact on the conversation.
- Don't argue a point to show you are always right.
- Don't try to outdo others. Conversation works better when cooperating, not competing.
- Don't use put-downs. It doesn't do you any favors and hinders communication.
- Don't talk to just one person, use inside jokes, or exclude people in other ways.
- Don't present yourself as a very nervous person; it makes others feel nervous, too. Instead imagine you are with a good friend, having an at-ease conversation. Continually work on bringing yourself to a relaxed state.
- Don't talk in a way that's hard to understand, for example speaking too fast, covering your mouth with your hand, or mumbling.
- Don't be a Grammar Nazi and start correcting people's grammar. Nobody likes it!
- Don't tell people about your personal life as soon as you've met them. Build a connection before you start opening up.

- Don't talk to people when they don't want to talk. Sometimes people are not in the mood for conversation.
- Don't give backhanded compliments, for example, "That's a nice dress you're wearing. It almost fits you."
- Don't take someone's viewpoint and twist it so that it falls at the extreme end of the continuum. For example, if a person says "I don't like fried foods," avoid replies along the lines of, "Oh, so you only eat health foods then, and look down on others who don't?"
- Don't humiliate others. For example, "You used to wear clothes like that when you were very overweight, didn't you?"
- Don't talk about weird things with people you don't know well!

2. ANSTCODE

ANSTCODE? OK, so I made it up.

AN-ST-CO-DE is, however, a useful acronym to help you remember four aspects of effective communication:

ANalysis
STructure
COntent
DElivery

ANalysis

Consciously or subconsciously, good conversationalists will carry out a quick analysis of the situation and the people there.

When they go into a situation, they may note what the energy in the room is like—is it making people feel happy, relaxed, excited, antagonistic, quiet? They may notice the level of formality of the situation and of people's interactions—how well do people seem to know each other and how relaxed are they in each other's company? They may pick up on individual people's moods and emotions. They may roughly work out the personality types there and get a feel for how they communicate. If they can't work it out or don't have time, they may ask, for example, "Are you feeling OK today?" or "Have I walked in at an awkward moment?"

Not all people are sensitive to these kinds of issues, however, especially "I-people" who are more self-focused. Those who work toward being "You-focused" and carry out a brief analysis of the people and the situation find it will lead to better conversations.

STructure

Structure of a conversation

Conversations have a basic structure—as with most types of communication—of an Opening, a Body, and an Ending. In conversation, this can at times be flexible.

The Opening is short and is typically a greeting, "Hello, good to see you," or a question, "Hi, how are you?" At times, usually in an informal situation where people know each other well, the Opening may not occur, and people may move straight into the Body.

The Body comprises the essence of the interaction and involves turn-taking.

The Ending can be "agreed" on by those present when the topic has run its course, may be determined by time factors, or may end when one person notices that the other is no longer engaged in the topic. The Ending is usually short and comprises some form of wrap-up and "goodbye" utterances. In a group, this may not happen if someone simply leaves the conversation.

Structure of a response

In addition to adhering to the overall structure of a conversation, good conversationalists may work out the structure of the responses they give during the exchange.

Before responding to a question or a topic, they may roughly formulate their reply by choosing an end point—message or purpose of what they want to say—together with the points along the way to support this.

Alternatively they may use a speaking framework to provide a structure to their response, for example, a Past Present Future framework. In this case they would talk about what happened in the past, what is happening now, and how they see it working out in the future.

COntent

The content is the words that people say, namely what they contribute during the conversation.

Good conversationalists generally like to ensure that what they say is:

- Relevant to the topic. They stay on-topic, make appropriate contributions at appropriate times during the conversation, and avoid unnecessary interruptions.
- Relevant to the people. They talk at the right level for the people present—for example, not too complex nor too simplistic—slow enough if people are not familiar with the language, and at the right level of politeness and respect.
- Relevant to the situation. They take into account the formality of the situation, if there are sensitive issues they should avoid, and if they need to speak at a certain volume.

- Of the right length. They give enough detail, not too little nor too much.
- Of the right clarity. They give clear explanations or instructions.
- Of the right value. They are honest, have credibility, and speak with a level of knowledge that supports their message.
- Framed well. They give a frame of usefulness and credibility to what they say.

DElivery

Delivery consists of how the verbal message—namely the words spoken—is conveyed, and comprises the visual aspect (what people see) along with the vocal aspect (how it is said).

Good communicators look and sound:

- Confident and competent. They display a pleasant level of confidence via their body language, use of words, and tone of voice.
- At ease. They know that if someone looks and sounds ill-at-ease, others will tend to feel the same, so they aim to look relaxed and comfortable when speaking to help others feel at ease.
- Enthusiastic. They know that enthusiasm is contagious and that people like to listen to people who look and sound passionate about their topic. Good communicators can help people find almost any topic interesting via the use of their enthusiasm.
- As if they relate to the people they are talking to. They may, for example, smile, use the other person's name, turn to face them, and talk about topics in which they know the other person is interested.

3. Quirky

Quirky can be defined as "having or characterized by peculiar or unexpected traits or aspects."

Conversation starters

The quirky conversation starters have been devised to give you the opportunity to address topics or talk about concepts that may not crop up in your average day-to-day conversation.

Not all of the starters may be deemed to be quirky. They fall on a continuum, ranging from slightly unusual though hopefully interesting starters, such as "Why does hair go gray when we get older?" through to quirky starters such as, "What could be the benefits of hanging your washing on the line in alphabetical order" and everything in between, in order to give a balance. All the starters, however, should provide the chance for you to give creative answers or use your creativity to work out solutions to questions you haven't thought about or don't already have the answer to.

You can choose the type of response you give, from quirky to non-quirky replies. You don't, for example, have to give a quirky answer to a quirky question. Your response to the above question may simply be, "Hanging the washing on the line in alphabetical order would make people who pay undue attention to detail feel very comfortable."

You could give a quirky answer to a non-quirky question: "People's hair goes gray as they get older because they start to identify with long-living animals such as elephants and want to mimic their color." This kind of response may provide some humor and will certainly allow for thinking in a non-traditional way.

Be aware, though, of straying too far along the continuum of responses, and avoid ones that may be deemed to be bizarre or distasteful if you want your conversation to appeal to the majority of people.

Although the starters may be quirky, the conversations don't have to be strange or weird. They may fall into a wide range of conversation types, including highly intellectual, fun, humorous, serious, and creative—in fact, all types of conversation.

General conversation

In general conversation, situations may arise that lend themselves naturally to quirky conversation openers. For example, some items, or the environment, can act as a catalyst for interesting lines of conversation. Let's say you met someone wearing a red and yellow-striped shirt and a green and blue spotted bow tie. Those items of clothing would most likely constitute the start of a conversation. Or if you went to someone's house and they had pairs of shoes glued to the wall, it would be hard not to mention them. Or if a colleague turned up to a meeting with a large box of pink fluffy ski hats, you would want to know the story behind it.

How quirky is too quirky when it comes to conversations?

There is no hard and fast rule; it mainly depends on the context.

When I told a friend about this book, she said to me "I wouldn't want to go up to someone I didn't know and ask a quirky question." I generally wouldn't want to either! The starters in the book are mainly for use with people you know or when you are with people in general conversation. They weren't devised to accost strangers on the street with . . . though to each their own!

However, some of the more ordinary ones can be used with new people you meet, and—if the situation is right— some of the quirky ones may be OK to use too. Just ensure you have a good reading of the situation if you don't want to alienate others, cause an unpleasant atmosphere, or be seen to be somewhat eccentric. Unless you are eccentric!

Some factors to be aware of when reading the situation:

- Different personality types. As a generalization, people's personality type falls into one of four categories, with most people being a mix of two or more: Outgoing, loud, fun loving, talkative, little interest in detail; determined, organized, goal- and task-focused, born leader; easy going, patient, well balanced, good listener, people-focused; serious, purposeful, deep, thoughtful, analytical, neat and tidy. If you can get a sense of the personality, you'll get a sense of how open they are to quirky conversations.

- How well you know someone. If you know them well, it will be easier to make the judgment call, if you don't know them well, be aware that some people take a while—or the right circumstances—for their true personality to emerge, and what you see on the surface may not be a good representation of what they are really like.

- The general situation. A formal meeting in a boardroom will lend itself to different ways of thinking, behaving, and conversing than a house-warming party, for instance. Each situation comes with an unspoken set of expectations, so be careful to read the situation well.

- The nature of the topic. Some topics lend themselves to being light hearted, for example, "Can you think up three new and unusual flavors of potato chips" or "Life would be fun if you and I had the powers of a super-hero, right?" Some, however, may have the potential to bring out more serious issues, for example, "If there could be only one religion in the world, which would it have to be and why?" or "Do you believe it when people say they are not racist?"

- Timing. Being very quirky may be perfectly acceptable, but it may not be appropriate until later on when the conversation has warmed up. Introducing something quirky to a cold conversation may not always work.

- Whether people see things the way you do or not. Sometimes a person might consider something to be light hearted, quirky, and amusing, while another person might consider it to be strange or in poor taste. People see things differently. This is the beach ball concept we talked about earlier, where several people may encounter the same thing yet regard it differently. For example, one of the topics is "An innovative way to reduce the gap between rich and poor is to . . ." A light-hearted response may be to say ". . . find a Robin Hood figure and pull together a band of Merry Men." Someone who works with people living in poverty may find this an inappropriate and upsetting response to a serious issue.

DEVELOPING CREATIVE THINKING AND PROBLEM-SOLVING SKILLS

Being able to think in new and different ways and look at problems from a different angle can bring many benefits. When we come across new situations—situations where the usual strategies aren't appropriate or where traditional thinking doesn't address the issue—being able to employ a new and different way of thinking can often help us solve problems and reach our goals.

If we become entrenched in our habits, we can become entrenched in our thinking. If routine plays a large part in our life, it can dampen even the sharpest of minds. To address this, we can move away from some of our habitual actions and routines to help expand our creativity and thinking skills. A range of suggestions is listed, suggestions that will stimulate the brain and keep it lively and active. They are not the only options, however, so feel free to add some of your own.

Carrying out any of the suggestions once or twice won't make a difference, but if you start to regularly take actions of this nature, you'll be training your brain to widen its horizons and develop your creative thinking skills and problem-solving abilities.

Creative thinking

Create the right conditions

The ideal conditions for thinking creatively vary from person to person, so choose the optimum environment for you. It may be total peace and quiet in a warm room, listening to music, sitting in a room with mood lighting, having a deadline, working on your own, or working with someone else.

If the conditions aren't right for you, it could produce the opposite effect and your creativity may be suppressed.

Trust in yourself

Even if you don't feel creative, it's said that we all have creative ability, and you may be using your creativity without even realizing it. You may, for example, devise a new recipe, choose and arrange the furniture in an aesthetically pleasing way, have the skill to style your daughter's hair, or be able to write an interesting email or memo.

Trust that you have an innate ability to be creative. If nothing comes to mind, don't put pressure on yourself; simply leave it for a while and allow the ideas to come when they are ready.

Ideas have a habit of happening at unexpected times, perhaps when you are out for a walk, in the bath, or about to drop off to sleep, for instance. Devise a way of making a note of these, for example, by keeping pen and paper on the bedside table or by using your cell phone to write a memo or record yourself speaking.

Change a routine

Vary some of your routines so you don't go into automatic pilot. Do you shower, get dressed, have breakfast? Could you shower, have breakfast, and then get dressed? Do you come home and watch TV every Friday? Could you instead ask a friend round and cook a meal together, or read a book, or do some DIY? Do you get up in the morning, access the Internet, and check your emails? Could you get up, do some gentle exercise, get ready, and then check your emails? Any changes in routine can help keep your brain active.

Sit in a different seat

Most people seem to be creatures of habit and sit in the same or similar seat at home, at meetings, on the bus, at the dinner table. Sometimes simply sitting in a different seat will give you a different view and potentially a different way of looking at or thinking about something. You may find that you notice something different, and if other people have to move, too, they may also notice new things.

Take a different route

Often we travel to places using the same route and the same method of travel. Try varying it. Drive home down different streets, go visit your relatives taking a longer way round, park your car several hundred yards from your destination and walk down a new road to get there. Anything to break a habit.

To enhance the experience, make a mental note of what you notice when you go a different route.

Read something different (1)

Go to the library or to a book shop and borrow or buy a book or a magazine from a section you don't normally go to.

Then try reading it from different perspectives: think about what you get from it when you read it, if anything. Why would others want to read a book like that? What would *they* get from it? What would make them want to read another in the same genre? What made the author write it? What is their passion for the subject? What research did they have to do?

Read something different (2)

Read a part of a newspaper or magazine that generally wouldn't appeal to you. Read it well enough so you could have a discussion with someone about it.

Eat or drink something different

When food shopping, buy a type of food you have eaten before but have never bought; buy a type of food you have never eaten and learn how to cook it; find a different way of using the kinds of foods you already use; try out a new recipe; try unusual combinations of food or drink; when eating out order something that you have never tried; go to a different nationality of restaurant to the types you usually go to and try some of their food.

Juxtapose

Put very different things next to each other—items, ideas, thoughts, concepts. For example, the very old and the very new, the traditional and the non-traditional, the sensible and the ridiculous; a children's picture book next to a quantum mechanics book, an analogue time piece next to a digital time piece, a vintage dress next to a modern dress. Imagine Einstein next to Bill Gates, Abraham Lincoln next to Bill Clinton, Leonardo da Vinci next to Richard Branson.

What do you notice? What thoughts or ideas does it spark?

Find out about something new

Log on to the Internet, put your cursor in the search box, close your eyes, and type letters randomly. Follow some of the links it brings up.

Watch a short video (1)

Log onto the Internet, go to a video-sharing website, and watch a video on something you know little about.

Watch a short video (2)

Go to a video-sharing website, put your cursor in the search box, close your eyes, and type letters randomly. Watch one of the videos it brings up.

Learn something from other people

Ask someone who is knowledgeable on a topic you know very little about to explain it to you.

Learn a new skill

Enroll in a course to study something different in order to stimulate your brain. Have you thought about Japanese cooking, Feldenkrais, belly dancing, dealing with altitude sickness, special-effects makeup?

Look at an online forum

Think of a topic you know little or nothing about. Find an online forum and see what you can learn, not just about the topic but about the kind of people it attracts and their way of thinking.

Surround yourself with creative people

Mixing with creative people will be more beneficial to developing your creative thinking than surrounding yourself with traditional thinkers!

Plan

Take time to plan something you don't normally plan. For example: the weekly meals; a quiet weekend at home; how to spruce up the garden; a room-by-room spring clean of your house; evening classes you want to take over the next year; or a fitness regime.

Lyrics

Learn the lyrics of a song.

Learn the lyrics of a song in a different language.

Learn a list

For example: the ten tallest mountains in the world; the NATO phonetic alphabet; the winners of the Super Bowl for the last ten years; or the countries in South America. Or perhaps something longer, like a list of the elements in the periodic table.

Try singing the list! It can be an effective learning tool.

Avoid over-planning

When starting on a new venture or project, don't aim for perfection before you start. Grasp the essence of it, start with what you've got, and then make it better as you go.

Make something you haven't made before

For example: a greeting card; a cushion cover; a cork notice board; a coaster from popsicle sticks; a scarf; a stress ball; a mini hot house for growing seeds using a plastic drink bottle and a plant pot; a video; a podcast.

Write *anything*

If you decide to write and find you have a version of writer's block, write down just anything at all. Then leave it for a while and come back to it. It may spark other ideas. It may also let you know the track you shouldn't be going down.

Go against the flow

Think of some of the current trends and work out a way to effectively do the opposite. For example, what's a good alternative to: being connected via technology all the time; eating breakfast, lunch, and evening meals; owning a home; saving for retirement; keeping up to date with the news; or buying from supermarkets? You don't necessarily have to do them; the act of thinking them through will serve to hone your creativity.

De-clutter

Get rid of unwanted mess to free up space in your head for being creative. Do it in short bursts if you like: the bathroom cabinet; the compartments in your vehicle; your purse; your inbox; a bookshelf; a kitchen cupboard; under the bed; or the shelves in the closet.

De-clutter and be inspired

When you are de-cluttering and come across items you had forgotten about or didn't know you had, work out ways they may be useful, either in a traditional or a non-traditional way, for yourself or for someone else.

Turn it around

Take a picture, painting, or photograph and turn it upside down. Imagine that it's meant to look like that and work out what the artist or photographer was trying to get across.

Do a drawing upside down

If you turn a picture upside down and then copy it, it can help stimulate the right side of the brain. Start with a fairly simple line drawing.

Instead of seeing what you expect to see, you will need to develop your skills of observation—things don't look familiar when they are upside down. You will see combinations of lines and shading rather than familiar shapes.

Meditate

Give yourself and your mind a break from the busyness of life. As you let your brain reach a peaceful, calm level, you are more likely to become aware of the creative thoughts that were previously hidden to you.

Through regular meditation you can train your mind to focus and to access the creative space more easily.

You can choose your own form of meditation or use guided meditations and meditation music specifically for creativity.

Hand-eye coordination

Do something that involves developing your hand-eye coordination, like throwing a ball into a container from a distance, learning a coin trick, hitting a ball with a bat, or doing a jigsaw.

You could also try these with your non-dominant hand.

Go somewhere else

Come out of your usual environment and allow your mind to be stimulated by new images, sounds, and smells. Go to the beach, to a forest, on a train, the kind of café you would never go to, the zoo, an old church, a graveyard, a busy shopping mall, a museum, on a ferry ...

Talk to extreme people

Talk to quirky people, eccentric people, highly successful people, uncompromising people, snobbish people, condescending people, imaginative people, goofy people. You can gain inspiration from people with very different viewpoints.

Take a break from being sensible

What is the safe, sensible way to do something? OK, now work out the impractical way to do it. It will require you to try a different kind of thinking.

... Or take a break from being impractical

If you generally aren't sensible, have a go at that for a change! What might be the sensible alternative to the way you usually do something?

Ask questions

Sometimes our creativity may be blocked, and we find it hard to think up new ideas. One of the ways to deal with this is to ask relevant questions. If using the starter "What can you suggest that would make having gray hair appear fashionable?" try asking a few questions. For example: Who has gray hair and is fashionable? How have they managed that? Who has gray hair but isn't fashionable? What's the difference? When do people with gray hair get described as fashionable?

Using Who, What, Why, When, Where, and How questions will usually get the ideas flowing.

Passwords

Try using different passwords for all your apps, accounts, and so on. It will stimulate the brain into thinking up new passwords—and in a format you are likely to remember them—as well as the process for remembering them.

Come out of your comfort zone

Keep your brain active by undertaking activities that take you out of your comfort zone. Can you offer to speak at the next staff meeting; make contact with a neighbour you haven't yet spoken to; organize an event; design a poster; redecorate a room in a different style; or learn a new sport?

Use your non-dominant hand

Your dominant hand is linked to the opposite side of the brain, so if we spend time using our non-dominant hand it can stimulate the other side of the brain.

Our right brain is generally deemed to be associated with creativity, intuition, thoughtfulness, perception, and emotions, while our left brain is associated with logic, language, numbers, intellect, and reasoning.

As it's not so common to undertake activities where we use both hands, our dominant hand does most of the work. Some studies show that we activate one hemisphere when we use our dominant hand but activate both when we use our non-dominant hand.

How can we use our non-dominant hand? How about: writing the alphabet; drawing a simple picture of a house; tracing over a drawing; brushing your teeth; doing household chores such as pegging out the washing or dusting; making something with toy bricks or play dough; dealing playing cards; combing your hair; turning the pages of a book . . .

When developing any new skill, note that there will be aspects you find challenging and frustrating, and you will think you are going backward, but perseverance is everything!

Problem-Solving

See it from another's viewpoint (1)

Talk to someone very different from you and ask how they would go about solving the problem. It could be someone much older, much younger, from a different culture, from a different background, from a different line of work, or a child.

Their life experiences and ways of thinking may shed a new light on the issue and allow you to see it from a different angle. Being able to think in a different way may provide the start of a solution for you.

The other person may not even see it as a problem, and may in fact help you see the issue in a positive or different light.

See it from another's viewpoint (2)

Imagine you are someone else, a completely different person, real or imagined, and think about how they would tackle it.

For example, how would Bill Gates tackle it? Oprah Winfrey? Barack Obama? Donald Trump? Lady Gaga? Captain

Kirk? Your neighbour? One of your high school teachers? The Chief Exec in your workplace? Your auntie? The founder of a supermarket chain? The president of your sports club? A psychologist? Your doctor?

See it from another's viewpoint (3)

Research how people in different disciplines have dealt with similar issues. If it is a work problem, for example, explore how other industries have tackled the same or similar issues. They may have approached it from a different angle, found a very simple solution, changed tack, or used different instruments or technologies. Analyze what they have done and see how it can be applied to your situation.

See it from another's viewpoint (4)

How do different cultures or countries deal with the same issue? We can get so used to the cultural norms that surround us that we may not be aware of completely different ways of looking at issues and solving problems. Examine different countries' cultural perspectives.

How, for example, might someone from East Africa deal with the issue of losing weight; what might someone from China view as a good way to amend the school curriculum; what strategy might someone living on a base in Antarctica adopt to keep fit?

What is the problem?

Take time to figure out what the problem *really* is. It may not be what it appears to be on the surface. What is the underpinning question?

Get an overview

Get to the heart of the issue and work out, on a scale of 1–10, how big the problem is. Having perspective will help with decision making.

In addition, ask yourself if you are doing anything, or if anything is currently happening, that can make it worse.

Avoid looking for people to blame

It's a waste of energy and time looking for someone to blame. There's a problem, so set about sorting it out.

Don't wait for someone else to sort it out

There's a problem, so set about sorting it out.

Get the best from brainstorming

One option is to ask people to brainstorm on their own first, and then come together as a group. This may prevent any domineering types having too much influence on the process and "squashing" the introvert types.

To brainstorm well, generate as many ideas as possible and write them all down, rejecting nothing. Then look at each idea in turn and consider its merits.

Brainstorm fast

Brainstorm as fast as you can without assessing the ideas, simply letting them flow. Set yourself a time frame, for example, fifty ideas in five or ten minutes. You can evaluate later.

Devise a ridiculous solution

Ask yourself, "What is the most ridiculous way to solve this problem?" Brainstorm on your own or with others and write everything down, no matter how ridiculous or off-topic. When finished, analyze and adapt any ideas that look like possibilities. A quirky suggestion may end up being the best solution or a catalyst for useful ideas.

Devise an impossible solution

Ask yourself, "What is an impossible way to solve this problem?"

Nelson Mandela said "It always seems impossible until it's done," and what might have seemed impossible at one point in time may now be very commonplace. Perhaps you could be a leader in doing something in a completely new way.

There may be more than one solution

If people hold the belief that there is a *right* way to solve a problem or that there is only one solution, then it is likely to hinder creative thinking and problem-solving ability. Many issues have more than one possible solution. As the old saying goes, "There is more than one way to crack a nut."

The learning process

It's useful to remember that the process of learning may very well include experiencing attempts that don't work. They are not necessarily mistakes; they are an integral part of the learning process. In the words of Thomas A. Edison, "I have not failed. I've just found ten thousand ways that won't work."

Push yourself to the edge

When we push ourselves to the limits of our ability, we take a risk. We may fail. That's OK, it has simply shown that we have gone further than our level of competence for the moment and is giving us the opportunity to learn a bit more.

Failed?

Have you failed somewhere along the way so that you now have a problem? Don't worry. In the words of Henry Ford, "Failure is only the opportunity to begin again more intelligently." The most successful people have failed, and usually failed many times. What makes them successful is that failure holds no fear for them, and that they don't give up when things become challenging.

Failure doesn't generally happen in one fell swoop; failure is usually the result of small behaviors that are repeated regularly. Look back to the beginnings of the problem. What are the behaviors—and the beliefs that led to the behaviors—that have taken things off track? What are alternative, and more effective, behaviors to adopt?

Write a haiku of your problem

Can you express your problem in a different and creative way, for example, with a poem? Writing poetry engages a creative part of the brain and can help you think about the issue differently.

A haiku is a short seventeen syllable poem. It consists of three lines, where the first line has five syllables, the second has seven, and the third has five.

For example, if your issue was, "I don't like working long hours," you may express this in a haiku as:

Monday to Friday
Too many working hours
My kids losing out

Write a longer poem of your problem

If a haiku is too short for you to express the issue, write a longer poem either in rhyming or free verse.

Draw a diagram of the problem

Get a sheet of paper and draw a diagram or picture of the issue. It will tap into your creative thinking mode and allow you to see it in a different way. Use colors to illustrate the different aspects of the problem.

Write down or draw the problem using different materials

Use something different to write on, such as wallpaper, aluminium foil, a beer coaster, the inner side of a cereal box, a window, or an old shirt.

Use something different to write with: chalk, lipstick, a small paintbrush dipped in ketchup, a large paint brush and a tin of purple paint, a typewriter, erasable marker pens. Or go to the beach and draw it in the sand.

Taking ourselves out of our usual way of problem-solving may lead to innovative solutions.

Discuss the problem in a different environment

Instead of the usual sitting round a table, you will most likely think differently if you change the environment. Can people sit under the table; sit with their backs to one another; sit in the dark; sit or stand under a tree; sit in the car overlooking the sea; sit on cushions in a circle ...?

Give yourself boundaries

When people have too much freedom to mull over an issue it can be difficult to narrow things down, so set parameters to allow for focus.

For example, give yourself a time limit of ten minutes to brainstorm; or think of eight ways to de-clutter; or write down possible solutions on a 6" by 6" piece of paper; or only look at one very small part of the issue.

Work out an interesting solution ...

... and then make the problem fit the solution. For example, you might decide the solution is "42," or "a week on Tuesday," or "Chicago," or "a bag of apples." How do you then get from the problem to that solution?

What's your gut feeling?

Some studies show that following your intuition and making a decision based on instinct can often be the best decision, as it is based on our own innate wisdom. It's especially useful when you don't have time to do the research and weigh up all the pros and cons.

A hunch, a whim, or a strange urge could all be giving us helpful, "higher level" messages. And the more we honor the messages we are getting, the more we can develop our intuition and the more we can deliberately tune in to it.

What's the size of the problem?

Alternatively, for minor decisions, you could take the time to weigh up all the pros and cons. For large, life-changing decisions, let the answer come from deep within yourself.

Address emotions

If the problem is causing you to feel emotional, take steps to address the emotions; move away from the problem and allow the feelings to subside. Then look for strategies to deal with the emotions. Being in a highly emotional state will lead to less-effective choices.

Coming from a state of calmness will lead to more effective decisions. It will allow you to listen to your gut feeling, if that is what you want, and will allow for clearer thinking.

Advice from others

If you have taken advice from others, you will probably find that some aspects are suitable and some aspects are not. Work out which parts of it you identify with and feel you can benefit from.

Break it up

When a problem seems large and overwhelming, take heart in the knowledge that you don't need to deal with it all at once. You can break it up into bite-sized chunks, separating it into its different components, and tackle them one at a time.

Apps

There are numerous apps for problem-solving, creativity, and creative thinking. They can help you generate ideas, organize them, reshape and finish them, and more.

Imagine someone asking you ... (1)

If you are facing a problem or issue and are unsure of the next step, imagine saying to someone, "I don't know what to do" and they reply, "Well if you *did* know what to do, what would you do?" This moves the brain into a different mode of thinking.

Imagine someone asking you ... (2)

In situations where problem-solving is proving challenging, instead of focusing on what you can't do, imagine instead someone asking you why you *can* do it. The operative word is "why," and your response should begin with "Because ..." This again moves the brain into a different mode of thinking.

For example:
"I don't know who to ask for advice."
"Why are you good at knowing who to ask for advice?"
"Because ..."

Imagine someone asking you ... (3)

Imagine that a friend asked you for advice on solving the same problem you have. What advice would you give? Taking a disconnected view of the issue can give you a different perspective on it.

After the problem

Imagine you have already solved the problem and have been asked to give an explanation of how you did it. You are looking back saying "I'm really glad that I ..." or "The way I tackled it was to ..."

Reframe

Sometimes, by reframing the problem at hand, it may cease to be a problem when viewed in a certain way. Alternatively, by reframing a problem, the route to take to address the issue may become clear.

Structured analysis

To avoid guesswork or trial and error, choose a structured method for analyzing the problem. It could be a set of questions you devise or a tried and true problem-solving strategy.

Take a break

When things get tough and you are making no progress, take a break, stop thinking about it, and do something completely different. Give your brain a rest and see what it comes up with when you are refreshed and it has had other stimulations. You may need a few minutes, a few hours, a few days, a few weeks. Maybe longer, depending on the problem.

Make different connections in the brain

Bring in some quirky thinking and let your brain go to where it wouldn't normally go. Introduce an off-topic concept and see where it takes you.

For example, if you are aiming to devise a new vacation, try bringing in disparate words such as "chimney pot," "cure for snoring," or "can opener." If you are suggesting ways to reduce spending, look at the concepts of the workings of an internal combustion engine, how children learn to read, or how the dinosaurs died out.

Going off on a tangent may lead you to an innovative solution.

Do exactly what you're not supposed to do

If you feel you can't make any headway, and as long as your actions are not illegal or harmful, try thinking and doing the complete opposite of what is required to see if you can remove any blocks.

Do a mirror drawing

This is an exercise in helping the brain adjust to new information. If you get it wrong in the beginning, that's OK; you will begin to adapt, learn, and become accustomed to a new way of looking at things:

Take a piece of paper, pen, and a small mirror. Draw a simple shape on the paper, such as a heart, a tree, or a house. Place the mirror upright behind the drawing and then draw over your shape, all the time looking in the mirror, not at the paper. Do it several times with the same or different shapes. You can progress onto words to trace over, and more difficult drawings.

To take it to the next level, use your non-dominant hand.

Don't "think outside the box"

Just get rid of the box.

Take a step

Even if you haven't worked out a complete solution, take a step forward. It provides impetus and trains you to do *something* rather than do *nothing*. Problems can rarely be solved by doing nothing. If you are taking steps in the wrong direction, people can help by pointing you in the right direction, or you can amend as you go. However, if there is no impetus, it is hard for people to help you. Think of the adage, "You can't steer a stationary car."

Decide to make friends with problems

What's your mind-set? Some people see problems as, well, problems. They don't enjoy them, they like to find someone to blame, and they let problems get them down. Other people see problems as a chance to make things better, and they simply get on with the task of solving them. They see life as an interesting journey full of problems and solutions and they make friends with problems. They see dealing with and solving a problem as a beneficial, fulfilling experience, a goal to be achieved. They know they will learn something along the way, build their resilience, and be able to pass on their knowledge to others.

Life is rarely without problems, so you might like to make friends with them.

Set a goal to be the best

When confronted with a problem, set a goal that you will solve it in the best way possible, that you will be able to look back and be proud of what you did, or that you and others will be impressed with the ability you showed when tackling the issue.

Maybe others will be so impressed with the ability you showed that you will be called on to share your wisdom.

Keep a log

Look back over problems you have solved in the past. Make a list of the problems, and insert them into a table with three columns. In the first column write what the problem initially appeared to be; in the second column write what the problem actually was, which may or may not be the same; in the third column write your problem-solving strategy.

Create a second list, one of problems you didn't solve, again with the same three columns. In this third column, you may find that sometimes your problem-solving strategy was "doing nothing."

Now do an analysis and see if is there a pattern. What do you notice about the strategies that worked and those that didn't? Did a strategy work in one situation but not another? Did you have to tweak a strategy to make it work? Did you use the same strategy in more than one circumstance? Were some strategies very simple? Were some multifaceted?

Be careful, however, that you are not lured into thinking that a previous technique or strategy will work in all situations. Different situations may need different approaches. It may be a new type of problem for which you need to find a new strategy.

Keep adding to the list as you encounter new issues. Being able to gain an overall picture of problem-solving strategies, and having an inventory of strategies to call on, may help you solve the next problem that crops up.

1,000 QUESTIONS AND CONVERSATION STARTERS

This chapter contains one hundred different topic sections, each containing ten questions or conversation starters. The topic sections are in alphabetical order.

Adverts	Create a Story
Age	Creative Solutions
Alternative Living	Dance
Alternative Reactions	Dating .
Alternative Uses	Dear Doreen
An Innovative Way To …	Describing People
Art	Devil's Advocate
Beach Balls	Devise an Ending
Being Creative	Different Dwellings
Being Rude	Different Endings
Big and Small	Dreams
Body Parts	Easier, Better, or
Books	Alternative
Career Choice	Education
Claims	Eight Hours
Clubs	Expertise
Combination Businesses	Explanations
Countries	Fast and Slow

Female and Male
Five Hundred
Food
For Hire
Health
Homes
How To
How Would You Use . . .
If You Were . . .
In Common
In the Style Of
. . . In the World
Interviews
Inventions and Innovations
Judging a Book by Its Title
Language
Life Would Be Fun If . . .
Marriage
Men and Women
Minimalism
Mixed Bag
Money
Music
Name Something or
    Someone
Neighbors
New Products
New Skills
New Year
Nothing
Odd One Out
Older People
One Hundred Years

Only One
Ordinary Situations
People and Situations
Pets and Animals
Photography
Physical Appearance
Post-nominal Letters
Quotes
Relationships and
    Romance
Semantic Fields
Stand in a Line
Stories with Messages
Tall Tales
The Body
Think Think Think
This and That
Time and Speed
Time Travel
TV
Unusual Concepts
Unusual Events
What Can We Learn
    From . . .
What   Could   Be   the
    Benefits Of . . .
What Would You Do If . . .
Who Is This?
Why?
Words of One Syllable
Work
Writing
You

You Can Do Anything!   Your Call!
You Walk into a Room
     And . . .

Plus . . . Your Favorites & Your Starters

Adverts

- Which celebrity would you use to advertise a campaign to bring back the use of typewriters?
- If you had to advertise a new type of denim jeans only via the medium of the radio, how would you do it?
- How could you entice people over the age of seventy to join the smartphone revolution?
- How would you advertise a "manly" form of dental floss to males in their twenties?
- How could slippers be advertised so they seem sexy?

> **(CO)** "Weird people don't care if they're weird. They are the most entertaining to converse with because nothing is off limits." *Donna Lynn Hope, author*

- What's a good way to advertise a self-help DVD to a teenage audience?
- Is it possible to advertise hair-care products using non-glamorous, ordinary-looking women in ordinary situations?
- How could you advertise the benefits of a bag that doubled as a sun hat?
- You have an old worn-out tractor sitting on your land that you need to dispose of. Even though it's rusty and doesn't work very well you don't want to give it away

for free. How could you advertise it so that someone would buy it?
- How could tea cozies be advertised to make them seem a trendy, must-have item?

(TD) "From now on, I'll connect the dots my own way." *Bill Watterson, author*

Age

- What age do you, on the inside, truly feel you are?
- Which year of your life would you like to relive?
- Why do children like getting older while adults generally prefer not to?
- Why are babies born at an age when they are helpless? Why aren't they born at an age when they can walk or talk, for example?
- Why is it usually seen as a good thing to reach the age of one hundred?

(CR) "Creativity is just connecting things. When you ask creative people how they did something, they feel a little guilty because they didn't really do it, they just saw something. It seemed obvious to them after a while. That's because they were able to connect experiences they've had and synthesize new things." *Steve Jobs, entrepreneur*

- Is it easier in society to be an old man or an old woman?
- When does middle age start and how long does it last?
- Medical advances have meant that we are living longer. Is there any point to this?

- Is there any benefit to retiring?
- At what age does a person become an adult?

(PS) "Difficulties are opportunities to better things; they are stepping-stones to greater experience. . . . When one door closes, another always opens; as a natural law it has to, to balance." *Brian Adams, author*

Alternative Living

There are many ways to gain fulfillment by doing something alternative. Can you explain the benefits of:

- Having no fixed abode and living a nomadic lifestyle.
- Not having a job or career.
- Making your own toiletries.
- Never going to the shops and instead ordering everything online.
- Taking a vow of silence for a month.

(CO) "Conversation about the weather is the last refuge of the unimaginative." *Oscar Wilde, author*

- Spending a year without buying anything new, apart from food.
- Living without a cell phone, computer, or TV.
- Having a husband or wife part-time.
- Not attending school during childhood.
- Working toward having little money, a non-busy lifestyle, and few possessions.

(TD) "Free thinkers are those who are willing to use their minds without prejudice and without fearing to understand things that clash with their own customs, privileges, or beliefs. This state of mind is not common, but it is essential for right thinking; where it is absent, discussion is apt to become worse than useless." *Leo Tolstoy, author*

Alternative Reactions

Give the usual reaction the average person may have in these situations and then give an alternative, but acceptable, reaction.

- A young woman with a small child approaches you in the street and asks for money to buy food for herself and her daughter.
- You are in a café and order a meal. You also ask for a glass of tap water and are charged the same price as for a cup of tea.
- You go home and find your house or apartment has been burgled.
- You check your lottery ticket and find you have won $100,000.
- A Jehovah's Witness comes to the door to discuss religion.

(CR) "Creativity involves breaking out of established patterns in order to look at things in a different way." *Edward de Bono, physician*

- You are running late for an important meeting. When you get to your car you discover you have a flat tire.
- It's Saturday morning, you have had a busy week and want to have a sleep in. At 7 a.m. the neighbors start doing very noisy DIY.

- You lose your cell phone and haven't backed up any of your contacts.
- You wait for two hours in a line to buy tickets for a concert that your twelve-year-old daughter is desperate to go to. The person in front of you buys the last tickets.
- Your employer is a week late paying your salary, the mortgage is due to be paid tomorrow, and you need the money.

(PS) "The most serious mistakes are not being made as a result of wrong answers. The truly dangerous thing is asking the wrong questions." *Peter Drucker, author*

Alternative Uses

These items have traditional uses, but could they be used another way?

- What else could you use a guitar for?
- What else could you use a sewing machine for?
- What else could you use a paintbrush for?
- What else could you use a watermelon for?
- What else could you use two house bricks for?

(CO) "Simply having the courage to say senseless things made me euphoric. I was free, with no need to seek or to give explanations for what I was doing. This freedom lifted me to the heavens—where greater love, one that forgives everything and never allows you to feel abandoned, once again enveloped me." *Paulo Coelho, author*

- What else could you use toothpaste for?
- What else could you use bank notes for?

- What else could you use underpants for?
- What else could you use bird seed for?
- What else could you use a toilet seat for?

(TD) "Men fear thought as they fear nothing else on earth, more than ruin, more even than death. Thought is subversive and revolutionary, destructive and terrible, thought is merciless to privilege, established institutions, and comfortable habit. Thought looks into the pit of hell and is not afraid. Thought is great and swift and free, the light of the world, and the chief glory of man." *Bertrand Russell, philosopher*

An Innovative Way To . . .

- Decorate your living room walls is to . . .
- Reduce the gap between rich and poor is to . . .
- Celebrate Christmas is to . . .
- Reduce water wastage is to . . .
- Spend two weeks' vacation is to . . .

(CR) "I doubt that the imagination can be suppressed. If you truly eradicated it in a child, he would grow up to be an eggplant." *Ursula K. LeGuin, author*

- Become famous is to . . .
- Reduce obesity is to . . .
- Write a book is to . . .
- Cook a rice or pasta dish is to . . .
- Display photos is to . . .

(PS) "[How to think about a problem:] The first step is to make the problem specific . . . ; The second step is to form theories freely of

how to rid yourself of that burden . . . ; The third step is to develop
in foresight the consequences of your proposals . . . ; The fourth and
final step in thinking is to compare the consequences of your proposals to see which is best in the light of your scheme of life as a whole
. . . ; Whether you choose a vacation or a spouse, a party or a candi-
date, a cause to contribute to or a creed to live by—think!" *Brand
Blanshard, philosopher*

Art

- The Statue of Liberty needs to be more in keeping with modern day sculptures. How do you propose to alter it?
- If the Mona Lisa had been painted to reflect twenty-first-century America, what would it look like?
- You are asked to produce a painting titled "Strange Adventure." What would the painting look like?
- You are asked to produce a painting titled "Liberty, Humor, and Greed." What would the painting look like?
- How could you take some paper tissues, a wire coat hanger, and a roll of string and make it into a piece of art?

(CO) "Good nature is more agreeable in conversation than wit, and gives a certain air to the countenance which is more amiable than beauty." *Joseph Addison, essayist*

- What is art?
- Art galleries all look the same! What's a better way of displaying art work?
- How many aspects do the works of Salvador Dali and Rembrandt have in common?

- If Picasso had painted the Sistine Chapel, what would it have looked like?
- Andy Warhol said "An artist is somebody who produces things that people don't need to have." Agree?

(TD) "The world we have created is a product of our thinking; it cannot be changed without changing our thinking." *Albert Einstein, physicist*

Beach Balls

Issues in life are often like beach balls—several people may look at the same thing yet see something different. Listed below are different scenarios, each with three types of people observing or participating. How might each person view the scenario?

- Scenario: A house is on fire. A woman jumps from a first floor window. Just as she is about to hit the ground, a person-sized shimmering light is seen near her, and she lands gently, without any injuries.
  People:
  A committed Christian
  An atheist
  A spiritual person

- Scenario: A six-year-old girl wearing false tan, fake eyelashes, hair extensions, and full makeup wins a US beauty pageant.
  People:
  The girl's mother
  A caseworker from Child Protective Services
  The mother of the girl who came in second

- Scenario: A hugely overweight person is standing in the line at a fast food restaurant ordering a very large meal.

People:
Another hugely overweight person
The proprietor of a slimming organization
Someone who has recently arrived from a third-world country whose fellow people are starving

- Scenario: A very large spider appears in a public building. A member of the public picks it up and puts it outside.
  People:
  Someone with a spider phobia
  A conservationist
  A psychologist

- Scenario: An elevator with three people in it breaks down for an hour.
  People:
  Someone who suffers from claustrophobia
  A potholer
  A relaxation teacher

(CR) "Trust that little voice in your head that says 'Wouldn't it be interesting if . . .' And then do it." *Duane Michals, photographer*

- Scenario: A very drunk man has fallen into a shop window, broken the glass, and cut himself badly.
  People:
  A worker from Al-Anon
  A policeman
  An ex-alcoholic

- Scenario: A new family has moved into a very upmarket suburb. They have recently won a large sum on

the lottery, come from a low socio-economic area, and present as rough and aggressive. They attend the community meeting.
People:
The chairperson of the residents' meeting
A social worker
A journalist from the local paper

- Scenario: A woman is going around a shopping mall. She has a broken leg, is using crutches, and is walking more awkwardly than would be expected.
  People:
  An orthopaedic surgeon
  A physiotherapist
  Someone in a wheelchair who does not have legs

- Scenario: A real estate agent is showing photos of a ramshackle cottage in a remote area.
  People:
  A city property developer
  A DIY enthusiast
  A person on the run from the police

- Scenario: Someone starts a new job and finds that the workload is very heavy, involves constant meetings and travel around the country, plus an expectation that they are to update their status regularly via social media.
  People:
  A hyperactive person
  A pensive person who believes that fast isn't always good
  A time-management specialist

(PS) "If you can't solve it, it's not a problem—it's reality." *Barbara Coloroso, author*

Being Creative

- What's the strangest question you have been asked about something you've created?
- Some people believe that to be creative you need to do the opposite of the norm. If you were a manager and wanted to bring creativity into your projects, what would be the benefits of celebrating failure?
- You have decided to bring a very specific and unusual theme into the décor of your bedroom. What theme would you like and how would you make it happen?
- Could you be inspired to be creative if you were in a cold, plain room with grey walls, grey shabby carpet, and a view over a derelict building?
- Your ten-year-old daughter has to go to school dressed as a famous person from history and has asked you to help. You are not allowed to buy anything and can only use what you have in your house. Who would she go as and what would you use?

(CO) "What frightens us most in a madman is his sane conversation." *Anatole France, poet*

- Have you found that when someone has a new, very creative idea, most people don't understand it straight away?
- Scott Adams said "Creativity is allowing yourself to make mistakes. Art is knowing which ones to keep." Are there any of your creative endeavours you shouldn't have kept?

- Some people believe that to be creative you need to do the opposite of the norm. If you were a manager and wanted to bring creativity into your projects, what would be the benefits of giving "lower status" workers "higher status" job titles?
- If five people were assigned to a project, all of whom were good at producing creative ideas but less effective at doing the work, what would happen?
- Some people believe that to be creative you need to do the opposite of the norm. If you were a manager and wanted to bring creativity into your projects, what would be the benefits of allowing people to have longer vacations?

(TD) "Invest a few moments in thinking. It will pay good interest." *Author unknown*

Being Rude

- Who would you most like to thumb your nose at?
- Why isn't it acceptable to emit body gases noisily?
- "May the fleas of a thousand camels infest your armpits" is an insult delivered by Klinger from *M*A*S*H*. Can you think of a better one than this?
- If there was an occupation called "insulter," what would this person do and which organization would they work for?
- According to the Urban Dictionary, iRude means the act of talking about your iPhone or Apple product in the presence of somebody that does not have one, or constantly using your iPhone or other smartphone when ostensibly socializing with other people. Choose another letter to go before the word "rude" and make up a definition for it.

> **(CR)** "When in doubt, make a fool of yourself. There is a microscopically thin line between brilliantly creative and acting like the most gigantic idiot on earth. So what the hell, leap." *Cynthia Heimel, playwright*

- If you could run in front of the TV cameras to blow a raspberry at somebody famous being interviewed, who would it be?
- In the Mr. Men book series, Mr. Rude says to an overweight woman "Fatty! You're supposed to eat the things in the fridge, not eat the fridge as well!" Why do people find things like this funny?
- What's so rude about bottoms?
- Burping is a sport! The World Burping Federation holds competitions to "celebrate those who show skill in the endeavor." How well would you fare in a burping contest?
- Paris is deemed to be one of the worst places for rudeness, and people who work with tourists have been given a booklet on how to improve their etiquette. If you were to produce a "How Not to Be Rude" booklet for people in your town, what would it include?

(PS) "Don't forget that some things count more than other things." *William Saroyan, dramatist*

Big and Small

- If you had to choose between being very tall or very small, which would you prefer?
- You have four weeks' vacation. Would you rather take all four weeks at once and have a big trip away, or would you rather take four separate weeks and have smaller trips?

- Would you like to have a partner who was a very different body size than you?
- Is it better for a small person to have a large dog, and a large person to have a small dog, to balance things out?
- Why do big, slow creatures such as elephants live much longer than small, fast creatures such as flies? And does this translate to humans?

> **(CO)** "A speaker should approach his preparation not by what he wants to say, but by what he wants to learn." *Todd Stocker, preacher*

- Is there any truth in the saying "The bigger the TV in the house, the smaller the collection of books"?
- Is there any truth in the saying "The bigger the earrings, the smaller the IQ"?
- In some cultures women aim to have big bottoms, as it is seen as attractive. Why isn't it this way in all cultures?
- Does the size of a person's statue, and the height of the plinth the statue is on, indicate their level of importance?
- It's said that we go through life aiming to have our needs met. Does it therefore follow that if someone has many needs they tend to create a big, full life, while someone with fewer, simpler needs can happily live a small life?

> **(TD)** "How wonderful that we have met with a paradox. Now we have some hope of making progress." *Niels Bohr, physicist*

Body Parts

- You have been commissioned to produce a painting or a set of paintings depicting "Hands across time and cultures." What would you produce?

- If you were to choreograph a dance called "Two left feet" how many people would you use and what would the dance look like?
- You are putting on a special musical production using singers, all of whom have different types of mouths and different types of voices. How many people would there be, and what kind of music would be appropriate for all singers to be involved in?
- The local hat shop is holding a fashion parade using people with different head shapes. They want you to be a model and ask you to describe your head shape and the type of hat that best suits you. What would you say?
- You have been asked to write an article on "special knees." Give an outline of your article and what the main message would be.

(CR) "Creativity is the sudden cessation of stupidity." *Edwin Land, scientist*

- You have been asked to draw pairs of eyes depicting seven different emotions: happiness, anger, love, boredom, tiredness, fear, and shock. What would each pair of eyes look like?
- If you could amend one part of your body and have it exactly as you wanted, which part would you change?
- Choose one of these internal organs and tell us as much as you can about its function: lungs, liver, heart, kidney, bladder, or stomach.
- Imagine that Noah was asked not to take two of each type of animal but instead to take two people of each body type. What kinds of people would he have taken on the ark?

- A New Zealand photographer is producing an exhibition entitled "Hongi." A hongi is a traditional Māori greeting where people press their nose and forehead to another person's. The photographer wants to use people with every type of nose. How many types of noses are there, and what are they like?

(PS) "Erroneous assumptions can be disastrous." *Peter Drucker, author*

Books

- If you had to classify all the books in a library into just three main categories, what categories would you choose?
- You have to write a self-help book giving the opposite advice than most of the others. What advice would you give?
- Which fiction book do you wish was real?
- Do you feel there is something missing? Is there a book that needs to be written but hasn't been yet?
- Choose one of your favorite novels and say what you would have done had you been the protagonist.

(CO) "The best kind of conversation is that which may be called thinking aloud." *William Hazlitt, author*

- What would happen if the characters from the book *Where the Wild Things Are* came alive?
- As well as creative writing, people can undertake creative reading. Can you give an example of this?
- Why aren't all books the same size so that people's bookshelves look neat and tidy?

- If Shakespeare's *Romeo and Juliet* were to be updated to reflect modern day culture, and both characters had cell phones, do you think the ending would have been different?
- Would authors of horror stories and crime novels be a bit scary to live with?

(TD) "It's not about breaking the rules. It is about abandoning the concept of rules altogether." *Paul Lemberg, business coach*

Career Choice

There are various theories about how people choose their career. Let's try a new approach. Let's imagine that you could look at someone and tell from their appearance the career they should really have. What career should these people have and why?

- The person you are talking to now
- Your mom
- Your dad
- Your sibling
- Your partner

(CR) "Creativity is a great motivator because it makes people interested in what they are doing. Creativity gives hope that there can be a worthwhile idea. Creativity gives the possibility of some sort of achievement to everyone. Creativity makes life more fun and more interesting." *Edward de Bono, physician*

- Your boss
- Your best friend
- Your other best friend
- Your son/daughter
- Yourself

(PS) "When fog prevents a small-boat sailor from seeing the buoy marking the course he wants, he turns his boat rapidly in small circles, knowing that the waves he makes will rock the buoy in the vicinity. Then he stops, listens and repeats the procedure until he hears the buoy clang. By making waves, he finds where his course lies . . . Often the price of finding these guides is a willingness to take a few risks, to 'make a few waves.' A boat that stays in the harbor never encounters dangers—but it also never gets anywhere." *Richard Armstrong, author*

Claims

Do you believe it when people:

- Say they have been abducted by aliens?
- Say they are the reincarnation of a famous historical figure?
- Say they can communicate with people who have died?
- Say that drinking lots of water is good for you?
- Say that there are no embellishments on their CV?

(CO) "People have to talk about something just to keep their voice boxes in working order so they'll have good voice boxes in case there's ever anything really meaningful to say." *Kurt Vonnegut, Jr., author*

- Say that there were a number of good aspects to Hitler?
- Say they don't care what other people think of them?
- Say they are not racist?
- Write on their Christmas cards that they'll contact you once Christmas is over?
- Say that man landed on the moon?

> **(TD)** "We are dying from overthinking. We are slowly killing ourselves by thinking about everything. Think. Think. Think. You can never trust the human mind anyway. It's a death trap." *Anthony Hopkins, actor*

Clubs

These are the names of fictitious clubs. What and who could they be for, and what would happen at their meetings?

- The B.A.D. Club
- The Shy and Retiring Club
- The Brown Cow and Yellow Duck Club
- The Daughters of Texas Club
- The Seven Seas and One Mountain Club

> **(CR)** "Don't think. Thinking is the enemy of creativity. It's self-conscious, and anything self-conscious is lousy. You can't try to do things. You simply must do things." *Ray Bradbury, author*

- The Gold and Platinum Club
- The Very Fussy Club
- The Wave Club
- The What Happened? Club
- The Me Me Me Club

> **(PS)** "Sometimes the situation is only a problem because it is looked at in a certain way. Looked at in another way, the right course of action may be so obvious that the problem no longer exists." *Edward de Bono, physician*

Combination Businesses

What could be the benefits of combining these businesses?

- A fast food outlet and a pharmacy

- A real estate office and a shoe store
- A gas station and a dentist
- A lawyer's office and a florist's store
- An exclusive dress store and a guitar maker

(CO) "As great minds have the faculty of saying a great deal in a few words, so lesser minds have a talent of talking much, and saying nothing."
François de la Rochefoucauld, author

- An IT consultancy and an art studio
- A cell phone outlet and an undertaker
- A life coaching business and a carpenter
- A dog grooming parlor and a vegetarian café
- A travel vacation business and a homeopath

(TD) "A conformist is a man who declares, 'It's true because others believe it'—but an individualist is not a man who declares, 'It's true because I believe it.' An individualist declares, 'I believe it because I see in reason that it's true.'" *Ayn Rand, novelist*

Countries

We all have an impression of what a country and its people are like even if we haven't visited it. What are your impressions of:

- Canada
- Scotland
- India
- Italy
- Russia/The Russian Federation

(CR) "The theoretician believes in logic and believes that he despises dreams, intuition, and poetry. He does not recognize that these three fairies have only disguised themselves in order to dazzle him. . . . He does not know that he owes his greatest discoveries to them." *Antoine de Saint-Exupéry, author*

- Saudi Arabia
- South Africa
- The Philippines
- New Zealand
- Argentina

(PS) "Responsibility is the most powerful internal motivator for problem solving. When you remove it, all that remains is the lesser drive of self-preservation. If necessity is the mother of invention then responsibility is its father." *Mark A. Crouch, author*

Create a Story

Use the following words and phrases to create a story, as probable or improbable as you like:

- FRANKENSTEIN – BLUE CHEESE – BENEFACTOR – ARMADILLO
- ENORMITY – REMOTE ISLAND – CHINESE DRAGON – FALSE BEARD
- HISTORICAL SITE – ELEPHANT TRAINER – BANSHEE – STRING QUARTET
- ROSE PETALS – ECCENTRIC MILLIONAIRE – CONTACT LENSES – FEROCITY
- LOST LUGGAGE – GARBAGE – ALTERNATE WEDNESDAYS – BONGO DRUMS

> **(CO)** "He's never quite got the trick of conversation, tending to hear in dissenting views, however mild, a kind of affront, an invitation to mortal combat." *Ian McEwan, novelist*

- PINE CONES – AWARD WINNING – DARK GREEN – EAR PLUGS
- PERFECT CIRCLE – ASTEROID BELT – MESSIAH – MAGAZINE
- BUDDHIST MONK – GOLDEN PHOENIX – CHEMISTRY TEACHER – SKIPPING
- LOVE HEART – PYGMY – ARCTIC CIRCLE – TELEVISION
- WATER SKIING – GRANDPARENTS – CHOCOLATE CAKE – NECKLACE

> **(TD)** "Impartial observers from other planets would consider ours an utterly bizarre enclave if it were populated by birds, defined as flying animals, that nevertheless rarely or never actually flew. They would also be perplexed if they encountered in our seas, lakes, rivers, and ponds, creatures defined as swimmers that never did any swimming. But they would be even more surprised to encounter a species defined as a thinking animal if, in fact, the creature very rarely indulged in actual thinking." *Steve Allen, television personality*

Creative Solutions

Can you think of ways to solve these problems creatively?

- You are an artist and have been asked to demonstrate to a group of fellow artists a unique painting technique you have devised. You travel several hundred miles, arrive at the venue where there are fifty people waiting, and discover your paints have been stolen. There are no other paints at the venue nor are there suitable stores nearby, though you have the canvases and brushes. What would you do?

- Your ten-year-old son Chris has written to his favorite children's TV program to apply to join in with a fun team competition. He's been accepted; you fly over on a Friday, check into a hotel in the evening, and go to the TV studios in the morning. You find out that it's an all-girl competition, the organizer hadn't realized that Chris was a boy, it's a live TV show about to air in an hour, and they don't want Chris to take part.

- You have booked an expensive, two-week romantic get-away with your wife on a beautiful, small remote island. You fly to the mainland then fly to a large island. The only way to get to the small island is to go in a canoe for a half-hour trip, which neither of you had realized. Your wife is terrified of traveling by canoe and refuses to go in it. There is no other way to get to the island.

- You are a natural therapy practitioner and have a specialist speaking topic, "A unique form of meditation for those with extreme phobias." You have been invited to give a presentation, but when you turn up you realize the organizer had misread your topic and has called it, "A unique form of *medication* for people with extreme phobias." The audience comprises doctors, physicians, and pharmacists expecting to hear about a new type of medication.

- You have agreed to house sit and look after a friend's house while she goes away for a month. You haven't seen her for a while, and when you arrive you realize she had neglected to tell you that she now has three cats you have to look after. You have developed a severe allergy to cats and are unable to live in the same house as them.

(CR) "Don't expect anything original from an echo." *Author unknown*

- You have been posted overseas for two months to a small town in a developing country. Your girlfriend is unhappy with you as you haven't been phoning her when you promised to. She has given you an ultimatum that you must phone the next day or else the relationship is over. You don't want this to happen, but the following day there is no phone or internet connection in the town where you are staying and you cannot work out a way to get in touch with her.

- You have opened up a new recording studio and are holding a launch in the evening. The studios already have several bookings starting the next day. Unbeknownst to you, one of your competitors attends the launch and sabotages your recording equipment.

- You have organized a surprise party for your three-year-old, have invited twenty children, and have arranged for a clown to come. You didn't know your child is afraid of clowns and they become hysterical and tell you to send the clown away.

- The organization you work for is having its twenty-first anniversary celebration and has ordered a huge custom-made cake that will be the focal point of the event. The press will be in attendance. You go to pick up the cake but when you arrive back, you trip and drop it.

- You have been going through a tough time and decide to go away for a week to have a break. When you come back you find that your friends have secretly redecorated your house to cheer you up. They have decorated it in a style you really don't like.

(PS) "The best way out is always through." *Robert Frost, poet*

Dance

- How could break dancing be adapted for people over sixty?
- If female tap dancers had to wear tutus and male tap dancers had to wear ballet tights, what would happen?
- What's the best form of dance for very overweight people?
- Imagine there was to be a ballroom dancing in blindfolds event. What strategies would dancers need to adopt?
- What would a hip-hop version of *Swan Lake* be like?

(CO) "Remember not only to say the right thing in the right place, but far more difficult still, to leave unsaid the wrong thing at the tempting moment." *Benjamin Franklin, founding father of the United States*

- If Fred Astaire and Ginger Rogers had been line dancers ...
- For those people who have two left feet and who struggle to dance, what's the nearest form of movement that could be classed as dance?
- How would the "Singin' in the Rain" dance sequence have to be adapted for the Argentine tango?
- In what way is life like dancing?
- Do you think that if God exists, he can dance?

(TD) "Men can live without air a few minutes, without water for about two weeks, without food for about two months—and without a new thought for years on end." *Kent Ruth, author*

Dating

- You arrange to meet for a first date at a cinema. When you arrive you find that your date is dressed as a superhero. What are some of the reactions you could choose to have?
- You want to take your date out in such a way that you will appear to be suave, sophisticated, and nonchalant. What would you do?
- Imagine you are a male called Fred. During the evening your date asks if she can call you Steve, as that's the name of an ex-boyfriend she used to like. How would you react?
- You are the owner of a supermarket and want to make Friday nights Singles' Night so that unattached people have the opportunity to meet each other. What would you organize?
- You attend an event where people take their ex-boyfriend or ex-girlfriend and "sell" their virtues to people who are looking for a new partner. How would you sell your ex-partner's good points?

(CR) "For me, insanity is super sanity. The normal is psychotic. Normal means lack of imagination, lack of creativity." *Jean Dubuffet, painter*

- If you were to advertise yourself on a dating site describing yourself as the complete opposite to what you are, what would you say?
- You want to take your date out in such a way that you will appear to be both intellectual and caring. What would you do?
- You have been asked to write an article titled "How to Be the World's Worst at Dating." What would you write?

- It's your first date with a new partner and you have invited them to your house for a cozy, homely afternoon in front of an open fire. They say they'd prefer it if you both went on a new assault course that's been opened up to the public. Is there a future for the two of you?

- You have been dating for some time and are getting on well. Your date invites you to meet their parents. When you go to their house you find they are naturists who like to walk around the house naked. They invite you to do the same. What are your thoughts?

(PS) "There are two ways of meeting difficulties: You alter the difficulties or you alter yourself to meet them." *Phyllis Bottome, novelist*

Dear Doreen

Imagine you are an agony aunt called Doreen who people contact because you give quirky but useful answers. How would you reply to the following?

- Dear Doreen, my identical twin brother has set up a Facebook page in my name and posts embarrassing photos of himself. People think it's me. What should I do?

- Dear Doreen, my wife's an acrobatic gymnastics tutor and says she will leave me to join a circus if I don't do some housework. I hate housework and feel it's a woman's job. Do you think she's serious?

- Dear Doreen, my fiancé says he wants to bring his best friend on honeymoon with us in case we have an argument, and then he won't have to spend time on his own. Do you think the friend should pay for his own flight and accommodation?

- Dear Doreen, I love my sewing machine more than I love my husband. I spend all day making beautiful garments for myself that bring me much pleasure. But a sewing machine doesn't pay the bills or get rid of spiders. My husband says I need to spend some time with him but I'd rather sew. What do you advise?
- Dear Doreen, is it wrong to eat breakfast in the shower?

> **(CO)** "The happiest conversation is that of which nothing is distinctly remembered but a general effect of pleasing impression." *Samuel Johnson, author*

- Dear Doreen, I am interested in one of the most fascinating topics in the universe—space ships. I read about it, watch documentaries, and contribute to many online forums. I have become very knowledgeable on the subject and can talk about any aspect of it at length. Surprisingly all the women I meet on dating sites can't converse adequately on this topic, so I must be using the wrong sites. Which dating site do you recommend?
- Dear Doreen, my mother and I have different views on the best way to hang washing out on the line. What are your views?
- Dear Doreen, I'm eighteen and a half. I want to get married on my nineteenth birthday, as all my friends got married then, and I have booked the church. I haven't met a suitable partner yet and so I need to know the quickest way to find someone.
- Dear Doreen, my neighbor has recently bought a Cadillac. Over the last year he has installed a pool and built a house extension. I've managed to keep up and do the same by maxing out on my credit cards but the banks won't lend me money for a new car. Where can I get the money from?

- Dear Doreen, my wife has a fascination for Santa Claus and wants me to be like him. I'm thirty-six, tall, slim with dark hair, work as a diesel mechanic, and would describe myself as "ambitious" rather than "jolly." What should I do?

(TD) "If everyone is thinking alike, then somebody isn't thinking." *George S. Patton, military commander*

Describing People

Take a tiny part of someone's life, build an entire personality around it, and describe what their whole life is like.

- People who like train spotting are . . .
- People who spend two weeks' vacation sunbathing on a beach are . . .
- People who watch lots of soap operas are . . .
- People who own Gucci handbags are . . .
- People who are fans of the British Royal Family are . . .

(CR) "I like nonsense, it wakes up the brain cells. Fantasy is a necessary ingredient in living, it's a way of looking at life through the wrong end of a telescope. Which is what I do, and that enables you to laugh at life's realities." *Theodor Geisel (Dr. Seuss), author*

- People who go moose hunting are . . .
- People who read palms and tell fortunes are . . .
- People who shop at thrift shops are . . .
- People who belong to a marching band are . . .
- People who spend a lot of time texting and tweeting are . . .

> **(PS)** "Success is relevant to coping with obstacles . . . But no problem is ever solved by those, who, when they fail, look for someone to blame instead of something to do." *Fred Waggoner, singer*

Devil's Advocate

Choose one person to play devil's advocate during the conversation. A devil's advocate is someone who takes a position he or she does not necessarily agree with, simply for the sake of debate. Do it in a light-hearted way!

- Has earth ever been visited by beings from other planets?
- Is it OK for men to wear pink clothes and an earring?
- Is it a good idea to let people take their pet into work?
- Is running and jogging the best form of exercise?
- Should we, as a society, have one day a year where we can do *anything* we like?

> **(CO)** "Ideal conversation must be an exchange of thought, and not, as many of those who worry most about their shortcomings believe, an eloquent exhibition of wit or oratory." *Emily Post, author*

- Does praying bring any tangible results?
- Is it OK to give children unusual names like Peachy Princess, Tangerine, Adolph, or Combine Harvester?
- Are tracksuits a better idea than formal school uniforms?
- Should every country have a royal family?
- What's the best thing to do when a pet budgie dies?

(TD) "If a man does not keep pace with his companions, perhaps it is because he hears a different drummer. Let him step to the music which he hears, however measured or far away." *Henry David Thoreau, author*

Devise an Ending

- There are only four ways to find a husband, including . . .
- The way to avoid losing an argument is . . .
- I would never be able to have a conversation with . . .
- I can solve most problems except . . .
- It must be great to be Chinese because . . .

(CR) "Sing in the shower. Dance to the radio. Tell stories. Write a poem to a friend, even a lousy poem. Do it as well as you possibly can. You will get an enormous reward. You will have created something." *Kurt Vonnegut, author*

- It's not a good idea to decorate your house in red and black because . . .
- If you listen to music before you go to sleep . . .
- People who can communicate with animals . . .
- The type of artwork to have in the bathroom is . . .
- If I could redistribute the amount of rainfall in the world, I would . . .

(PS) "One thing is sure. We have to do something. We have to do the best we know how at the moment . . . ; If it doesn't turn out right, we can modify it as we go along." *Franklin D. Roosevelt, US president*

Different Dwellings

- Your house is built on a base that rotates so that it can face any way you would like it to. How would you choose to use this feature?

- If apartments were designed so that any room could be interchanged with any other, how would you arrange your rooms?

- You have been offered the opportunity to have an additional room built onto your house, measuring 30' by 20' (9 meters by 6 meters). How would you use it?

- There are switches on the inside of all of your windows that allow you to have whatever view you would like from every window. How would you use this feature?

- If the place where you live was suddenly worth double the price for a limited time, would you sell it?

(CO) "There is no such thing as conversation. It is an illusion. There are intersecting monologues, that is all." *Rebecca West, author*

- If you can't already describe your house as "quirky," what would need to change so that it could be?

- Your entire house and contents have to be just one color. Which color would you choose and why?

- Your front door bell is set up in such a way that you can see who is at the door and can also send an electronic message that displays next to the bell, messages such as "Come straight in" or "Come back in an hour." If you could only have a choice of any six messages, which would you choose?

- Imagine there is a camera installed in your living room linked to a psychotherapist who could give feedback on what goes on. Would they be alarmed by what they saw?
- A distant relative decides to come and stay with you for a few weeks. He is an architect and criticizes your color scheme, furniture, and room layout and constantly tells you how to rearrange your house to make it more attractive and efficient. How long would he last?

(TD) "Discovery consists of seeing what everybody has seen and thinking what nobody has thought." *Albert Szent-Györgyi, physiologist*

Different Endings

Give a completely different ending to these stories or real events:

- *Cinderella*
- *Gone with the Wind*
- *The Lion, the Witch and the Wardrobe*
- The Nativity
- World War II

(CR) "Creativity is more than just being different. Anybody can plan weird; that's easy. What's hard is to be as simple as Bach. Making the simple, awesomely simple, that's creativity." *Charles Mingus, bassist*

- Princess Diana's life
- The moon landing
- Tutankhamun's life
- The Titanic
- John F. Kennedy's life

(PS) "If I had an hour to solve a problem and my life depended on the solution, I would spend the first 55 minutes determining the proper question to ask, for once I know the proper question, I could solve the problem in less than five minutes." *Albert Einstein, physicist*

Dreams

Have a go at analyzing these dreams and give your suggestions as to their meaning:

- You are floating above a park. It's sunny, children are playing, and people are having picnics. The scene is lovely and you wish you were part of it. You decide to float down and join in, but you start falling very quickly. Just before you hit the ground you wake up.
- You are on a small island where there is a beautiful castle made from crystal. Outside of the castle are aquatic birds, and you are able to choose one that will have a special meaning for you. You choose one that means "hope."
- You walk down a set of steps. At the bottom is a lake. A holy man wearing a wide brimmed hat brings a small boat and you get in. The man is silent, although you wish he would talk. He takes the boat into a dark cave where the opening looks like a big mouth. You can see a small exit in the distance but you can't get out and you start to panic.
- You are sitting on a hillside. It is a lovely sunny day. A man from a Native American tribe brings a large white buffalo and asks you to sit on it. He says he will take you to wherever you would like to go. You don't know which way, so you let the buffalo walk its chosen path.

- Your mother asks you to go get a gift for someone you know. You fly up and choose a rain cloud as it will give this person the freedom to release their tears as it releases its rain.

> **(CO)** "If you make yourself understood, you're always speaking well." *Molière, playwright*

- You dream of someone going to Paris, to the Eiffel Tower. They are scared as it is a long way away, but you know they will be safe.
- There is a group of strangers sitting around a fire, praying. You and two people you know decide to join them. You sit separately from each other. Each of you is invited to go for a walk with one of the strangers so you can ask them a question.
- A man in 1920s clothing comes to talk to you. He tells you his name and that he is a distant relative of yours. He wants to pass a message on to your father but you can't hear the message.
- You see your ex-partner who morphs into your current partner. You like him or her, you have lots of fun with them, but you know they could morph into someone else at any moment.
- You are watching a circus act and are especially interested in watching the fire-eater. There are lots of jugglers and circus clowns, but you are fascinated by the only fire-eater.

(TD) "It's OK to be wrong." *David Henry Hwang, playwright*

Easier, Better, or Alternative

- Is there an easier, better, or alternative way to help people in developing countries other than donating money to large organizations?
- Is there an easier, better, or alternative way to lose weight than to eat less and exercise more?
- Is there an easier, better, or alternative way for people to worship god without having lots of conflicting religions?
- Is there an easier, better, or alternative way to earn money than going to work?
- Is there an easier, better, or alternative way to learn life lessons without having to learn from your mistakes?

(CR) "It is better to fail in originality than to succeed in imitation." *Herman Melville, author*

- Is there an easier, better, or alternative way to have the possessions you want without having to buy them?
- Is there an easier, better, or alternative way to get people to like you without being nice?
- Is there an easier, better, or alternative way to get to know yourself than navel gazing?
- Is there an easier, better, or alternative way to look younger without plastic surgery?
- Is there an easier, better, or alternative way to be different than to have to be different?

(PS) "Never try to solve all the problems at once—make them line up for you one-by-one." *Richard Sloma, author*

Education

- You have been chosen to devise a new course for the country's school curriculum. What course would you devise for five to seven year olds?
- There needs to be more fun and laughter in schools! What could teachers do to bring more fun into the learning environment?
- You have been chosen to devise a new course for the country's school curriculum. What course would you devise for eight to twelve year olds?
- The education system needs a revamp. Children don't need to be in the same building five days a week, spending a lot of time sitting at desks, listening to a teacher and learning about subjects that don't always relate to life outside of school. This is my proposal for a completely different type of education system ...
- Instead of children of the same age being taught together, what are the benefits of having younger children sharing ideas with older children, and older children teaching younger children some of the time?

(CO) "It's no use of talking unless people understand what you say." *Zora Neale Hurston, author and anthropologist*

- You have been chosen to devise a new course for the country's school curriculum. What course would you devise for thirteen to sixteen year olds?
- If you had a teenage son or daughter and spent a day at their school taking part in all their classes, would you cope with the coursework?

- If some children want to leave school before the official school leaving age because they have—genuinely—more important things to do with their life, should they be allowed to leave?
- What would happen if there were no chairs in classrooms?
- Would it help if teachers came dressed in fancy dress costume from time to time?
- Albert Einstein said that education got in the way of his learning. Why did he say this?

(TD) "I can't understand why people are frightened of new ideas. I'm frightened of the old ones." *John Cage, composer*

Eight Hours

Many people's days are spent roughly split into three eight-hour segments—eight hours sleep, eight hours work or education, plus a further eight hours.

- If you had to spend eight hours watching movies, stopping only for food, bathroom breaks, and to change location if desired, what movies would you watch, how would you watch them, where would you watch them, and would it be difficult to maintain your enthusiasm?
- If you had to spend eight hours reading, stopping only for food, bathroom breaks, and to change location if desired, what would you read, how would you read it, where would you read, and would it be difficult to maintain your enthusiasm?
- If you had to spend eight hours talking to people on the phone, stopping only for food, bathroom breaks, and to change location if desired, who would you

talk to, where would you like to be, what might you talk about, and would it be difficult to maintain your enthusiasm?

- If you had to spend eight hours writing or drawing, stopping only for food, bathroom breaks, and to change location if desired, what would you do, where would do it, what might you write or draw, and would it be difficult to maintain your enthusiasm?
- If you had to spend eight hours doing some form of exercise or movement, stopping only for food, bathroom breaks, and to change location if desired, what would you do, where would do it, what physical challenges might you face, and would it be difficult to maintain your enthusiasm?

(CR) "Creativity takes courage." *Henri Matisse, artist*

- If you had to spend eight hours doing DIY on your house or the house of someone you know, stopping only for food, bathroom breaks, and to change location if desired, what would you do, where would do it, what physical challenges might you face, and would it be difficult to maintain your enthusiasm?
- If you had to spend eight hours driving or being driven around to look at scenery, stopping only for food, bathroom breaks, and to change drivers if desired, where would you go, what type of scenery would you like to see, and would it be difficult to maintain your enthusiasm?
- If you had to spend eight hours making something or some things, stopping only for food, bathroom breaks, and to change location if desired, what would you

make, what materials might you use, where would make it, what would the finished item(s) be used for, and would it be difficult to maintain your enthusiasm?

- If you had to spend eight hours in a sunny garden doing anything you liked, stopping only for food and bathroom breaks, what would you do, and would it be difficult to maintain your enthusiasm?
- If you had to spend eight hours searching the Internet for free items, stopping only for food, bathroom breaks, and to change location if desired, what device(s) would you use to access the Internet, what would you look for, what would the items be used for, and would it be difficult to maintain your enthusiasm?

(PS) "If you can't solve a problem, it's because you are playing by the rules." *Paul Arden, author*

Expertise

Due to your expertise in an unusual topic, you've been asked to share your wisdom on the following:

- How to train a goldfish
- Five ways to motivate your teenager to play the harp
- Interesting ways to write a name and address on an envelope
- Flower arranging without using flowers
- How to spot a British tourist at one hundred yards

(CO) "A conversation is a dialogue, not a monologue. That's why there are so few good conversations: due to scarcity, two intelligent talkers seldom meet." *Truman Capote, author*

- How to drive a car whilst looking cool
- How not to seem old when writing a text message
- How to choose the best tomatoes in the supermarket
- How to choose a dog that looks like you
- How to read a novel backwards and still make sense of it

(TD) "The individual has always had to struggle to keep from being overwhelmed by the tribe. If you try it, you will be lonely often, and sometimes frightened. But no price is too high to pay for the privilege of owning yourself." *Friedrich Nietzsche, philologist*

Explanations

What could be a possible explanation for these scenarios?

- The neighbor's ten-year-old daughter comes to your house and says, "My dad would like to borrow a vase, a bar of soap, and some olive oil."
- You go into a local antique shop to buy some candlesticks. The owner says, "I'm sorry but I can't sell candlesticks to anyone after three o'clock."
- You go to the shopping mall. People are walking around as normal but everyone is wearing red, blue, or white clothes.
- You go for a walk around the park. There is no dog show on but everyone is walking the same kind of dog.
- You order a subscription to a weekly magazine. Although you receive the magazine every week, the dates on them are random—some are from a few weeks ago, some from a few years ago, and some even have future dates on them.

> **(CR)** "Creativity makes a leap, then looks to see where it is. "
> *Mason Cooley, aphorist*

- Most days you receive a phone call at home from people wanting to reserve a room at "your" hotel. When you ask what number they have called, they all give a different number.
- Every day an old lady comes and stands near your house. When you ask why, she says she used to live on the street when she was a young girl. The woman comes across as mentally alert, but you live on a new estate and there were no houses in the area until ten years ago.
- A man walks into a hotel, gives the receptionist two empty milk cartons, and asks, "Are these the ones you are looking for?"
- A lady puts her best outfit on, climbs to the top of a nearby hill on her own, and sings at the top of her voice.
- All the evergreen trees in your neighborhood lose their leaves in the fall and regain them in the spring even though there have been no unusual weather patterns.

(PS) "The man who has no more problems to solve is out of the game." *Elbert Hubbard, author*

Fast and Slow

- You want to take a qualification that will allow you to move into a new occupation. You have the choice of doing it full time, without breaks, in eight months, or doing it part time, several hours a week over three years. Which would you choose?

- You are making a meal for four people: melon to start, then spaghetti bolognese, followed by fresh fruit salad. What is the absolute fastest time you could make these dishes in and what would you have to have in place to do it so quickly?
- Your neighbor comes round to tell you that she is getting her front door replaced and that the company has offered to replace your door at a 50 percent discount if you have it done today. Your door is old, though functional. Do you like making these kinds of decisions quickly or would you rather wait and pay 100 percent another time?
- If you were an animal, would you rather be a tortoise or a cheetah?
- Think about your current or most recent partner. Do—or did—you operate at different speeds?

(CO) "We reproach people for talking about themselves; but it is the subject they treat best." *Anatole France, poet*

- One of your colleagues, a single male in his forties, habitually goes home from work and watches TV in the evenings. At the weekend he goes shopping, goes for a walk, and tends the garden. He feels his life is too slow and he would like to live in the fast lane—just a bit. What would you recommend?
- When is a good time to listen to fast music?
- What is something you should never do slowly?
- What is something you should never do quickly?
- Human gestation lasts around forty weeks. What would be the effects if, instead, the usual time was twenty weeks or sixty weeks?

(TD) "We use 10 percent of our brains. Imagine how much we could accomplish if we used the other 60 percent." *Ellen DeGeneres, comedian*

Female and Male

- Should there be a check box on forms alongside the "Male" and "Female" boxes that is labelled "Other," for people who feel they do not fit the female or male definition?
- Do men and women drive differently?
- Is it true that men won't ask for directions if they get lost?
- Why are men hairier than women?
- Why are men usually taller than women?

(CR) "When we are angry or depressed in our creativity, we have misplaced our power. We have allowed someone else to determine our worth, and then we are angry at being undervalued." *Julia Margaret Cameron, photographer*

- Don't men need makeup as much as women?
- Why is there a stereotype of a dumb blonde?
- Is there any difference between men and women having tattoos?
- Is it OK for men to indulge in retail therapy?
- Why do women use a lot more toiletries than men?

(PS) "When I am working on a problem, I never think about beauty but when I have finished, if the solution is not beautiful, I know it is wrong." *R. Buckminster Fuller, architect*

Five Hundred

Imagine you have been given five hundred of the following items. You are not allowed to sell them, so what would you do with them?

- Canisters of silly string
- Tennis balls
- Chimney pots
- Pearl necklaces
- Roll-on deodorants

> **(CO)** "I particularly value conversations which are meetings on the border-line of what I understand and what I don't, with people who are different from myself." *Theodore Zeldin, author*

- Pairs of red socks
- Skipping ropes
- Soup spoons
- False mustaches
- Signed photos of Arnold Schwarzenegger

(TD) "The reasonable man adapts himself to the world; the unreasonable one persists in trying to adapt the world to himself. Therefore all progress depends on the unreasonable man." *George Bernard Shaw, playwright*

Food

- If you were wealthy enough to have your own personal chef, what types of food would you ask them to prepare?
- If 50 percent of the population of America chose to become vegetarian, what would happen from an agriculture and economy point of view?

- People eat animals such as cows, pigs, and sheep, but why don't people generally eat animals such as crocodiles, lions, and camels?
- How much of the average person's diet would disappear if they weren't able to eat sugar?
- What type of food could a restaurant offer if it claimed to be offering completely different food from any other restaurant?

> **(CR)** "Creativity is not the finding of a thing, but the making something out of it after it is found." *James Russell Lowell, poet*

- Is there a market for a takeaway lunch bar for dieters that displays food based on its calorific value?
- Years ago it was predicted that food would be in pill form. Why hasn't this happened?
- Devise the world's most unusual sandwich.
- Is there a type of food that is good for making people laugh?
- Which vegetable would you describe as being a "ridiculous" vegetable?

> **(PS)** "The difference between what we do and what we are capable of doing would suffice to solve most of the world's problems." *Mahatma Gandhi, Indian leader*

For Hire

You would like to set up a business hiring out unusual services. Could you make money hiring out:

- A Pretend Husband, who wouldn't get bored when clothes shopping with a woman and would give helpful advice?

- Party Goers, for people who need more people at their party?
- A Diet Helper, who would come and give away all the food you are tempted to eat but shouldn't, whilst at the same time keeping you entertained in order to keep your mind off food?
- A Shoe Wearer, someone who wears and breaks in new shoes for you so they are comfortable when you start wearing them?
- A Friendly Dog for the times when people feel lonely?

(CO) "One way to prevent conversation from being boring is to say the wrong thing." *Frank Sheed, author*

- A Driver Advisor, who sits in the car with you and advises you on how to cope with back seat drivers and children who are over-energetic?
- A Personal Motivator, who turns up at your house in the morning and spends ten minutes with you working out your plan for the day and giving you a pep talk?
- A Daily Photographer, who takes a photo of you every day and compiles the photos into a keepsake album?
- A Checker and Mender, who comes to your house once every three months to check your vehicle and all the electrical items, and carries out repairs?
- An Activities Buddy, who takes you out once a month to try a new and interesting activity?

(TD) "Believing is easier than thinking. Hence so many more believers than thinkers." *Bruce Calvert, atheist*

Health

- Laughter is said to be a great healer. Create a Laugh-A-Lot program for hospitals that will bring laughter into the wards.
- If there are people who eat and drink all the wrong things, smoke too much, don't get enough exercise, but live to a ripe old age, why don't doctors recommend we follow their lead?
- For those people who don't find going to the gym or pounding the streets very interesting, what's a more exciting way to keep fit?
- Is it possible to devise a way for people to eat junk food and still be healthy?
- If eating isn't just about nutrition but is also about emotion, how could supermarkets sell "happy" food?

(CR) "The way to get good ideas is to get lots of ideas, and throw the bad ones away." *Linus Pauling, chemist*

- Some people don't find drinking water very appealing, despite the potential health benefits. How can we make drinking water more attractive?
- How can stores present vegetables in such a way that children would want to eat them?
- If we can have our tonsils, adenoids, wisdom teeth, tailbone, appendix, and sinuses removed with no adverse effects, what's the point of them?
- What could be the argument supporting the claim that wearing high heels regularly is good for women?
- What's an innovative way for people to eat more in order to lose weight?

(PS) "There are three ways you can get to the top of a tree: 1) sit on an acorn 2) make friends with a bird 3) climb it." *Author unknown*

Homes

- If you could have your home automated to do anything you like, what would you want?
- How would you design an apartment to accommodate an extremely tall man and an extremely small woman?
- Would you like a house in the shape of a pyramid?
- How would it make you feel if all the windows and doors in your house were made from curved instead of straight lines?
- What have a mud hut and a palace got in common?

(CO) "Surely only boring people went in for conversations consisting of questions and answers. The art of true conversation consisted in the play of minds." *Ved Mehta, author*

- If you could have an extra level on a house, would it be better to have an attic or a basement?
- When it comes to family homes, is bigger always better?
- People these days are too isolated. In order to move toward more communal ways of living, people need to . . .
- What's the best way to soundproof a house?
- The advantages of having a very large tree growing in the center of the house are . . .

(TD) "Few people think more than two or three times a year; I have made an international reputation for myself by thinking once a week." *George Bernard Shaw, playwright*

How To

Give your family and friends the benefit of your wisdom:

- How to strike a pose. When you are waiting in a queue, don't stand like everyone else. Here's my advice on how to strike a pose!
- How to get pumped. There are too many people being quiet and shy. Here's my advice for getting pumped and looking excited!
- How to be a slob. Sometimes we don't need to be smart, organized, or successful. Here's my advice on how to be a slob!
- How to be a world-famous creative person. Don't hide your light under a bushel, get out there and let people know how great you are. Here's my advice on how to use your skills to become world famous!
- How to wear quirky combinations of clothes. Why wear the same combination of clothes as other people? Here's my advice on how to put together any style of clothes and still look good!

(CR) "A new idea is delicate. It can be killed by a sneer or a yawn; it can be stabbed to death by a quip and worried to death by a frown on the right man's brow." *Charles Brower, copywriter and author*

- How to dance imaginatively. No more shuffling on the dance floor at the next family wedding, here's my advice on how to get people looking at you when the dancing starts!
- How to find the perfect partner. Forget dating sites and signing up for new hobbies; here's my advice on how to find the partner of your dreams!
- How to get on everyone's nerves. Fed up with being polite and kind to others? Here's my advice on how to be exceptionally irritating!
- How to write a killer CV. Everyone writes about their previous job history, qualifications, and skills. Here's my advice on how to produce an irresistible CV!
- How to hide at work. When things get busy and everyone wants your attention, here's my advice on how to make yourself undetectable!

(PS) "No problem can withstand the assault of sustained thinking."
Voltaire, author

How Would You Use ...

You have been given the following items and asked to make something creative out of them. What would you make?

- A large bag of potatoes, three yards of hessian, and ten newspapers
- Twenty red silk flowers, ten yards of pink ribbon, and a meter of thin silver chain
- A large tin of pink paint, fifteen drawing pads, fifteen envelopes
- A gallon of liquid chocolate, ten loaves of bread, ten pounds of salted cashews
- Three large palm leaves, a dozen coconut shells, fifty pine cones

> **(CO)** "Logic and fact keep interfering with the easy flow of conversation."
> *Mason Cooley, aphorist*

- Ten blue T-shirts, an American flag, ten green scarves
- Twelve balls of orange wool, twelve oranges, twelve pairs of orange gloves
- Six tractor tires, twenty vintage wooden crates, one hundred glass bottles
- A trailer-load of snow, forty golf balls, three window frames
- Sixty light bulbs, ten glass vases, thirty DVDs

> **(TD)** "Begin challenging your own assumptions. Your assumptions are your windows on the world. Scrub them off every once in a while, or the light won't come in." *Alan Alda, actor*

If You Were . . .

- If you were a tree or flower, what tree or flower would you be?
- If you were a ferocious animal, what ferocious animal would you be?
- If you were a country, what country would you be?
- If you were a painting, what painting would you be?
- If you were a book, what book would you be?

> **(CR)** "My alphabet starts with this letter called *yuzz*. It's the letter I use to spell *yuzz-a-ma-tuzz*. You'll be sort of surprised what there is to be found once you go beyond 'Z' and start poking around!" *Theodor Geisel (Dr. Seuss), author*

- If you were a song, what song would you be?
- If you were a recipe, what recipe would you be?
- If you were an item of jewelry, what item of jewelry would you be?
- If you were a newspaper, what newspaper would you be?
- If you were a musical instrument, what musical instrument would you be?

(PS) "When a problem comes along, study it until you are completely knowledgeable. Then find that weak spot, break the problem apart, and the rest will be easy." *Norman Vincent Peale, author*

In Common

Take any two from each list of words and see how many factors you can find in common between them.

- TEACHER – FROG – CAR – SKIN – BOWL
- LISP – BOTTLE – TOASTER – COURAGE – LEGS
- TONIC – FOX – PLANE – HUMANITY – SALAD
- PICNIC – SHED – BOAT – COPPER – CONCERT
- TRUMPET – FISHERMAN – CANDY – ELEVATOR – NAIL

(CO) "If you have an important point to make, don't try to be subtle or clever. Use a pile driver. Hit the point once. Then come back and hit it again. Then hit it a third time—a tremendous whack." *Winston Churchill, British prime minister*

- CHAIR – MANIC – LIGHTHOUSE – SAUSAGE – CONFETTI
- LISTEN – ISLAND – WITCH – MORTGAGE – LIMP

- TENNIS – CREAM – MONSTER – TRAIN – GOLD
- FREE – CAT – ROAD – PURPLE – NEWSPAPER
- HEAT – CLIMB – CAKE – STATUE – TATTOO

(TD) "Thinking is what a great many people think they are doing when they are merely rearranging their prejudices." *William James, philosopher*

In the Style Of

One of the ways to expand your speaking style, and help increase confidence, is to use the technique of acting as if you were someone else, or speaking in the style of another person.

Use these starters and speak in the style of a supremely confident speaker:

- These are my recommendations for making people in our country more caring toward fellow citizens ...
- The steps we need to take to make our local community more aesthetically pleasing are ...

Use these starters and speak in the style of a charismatic speaker:

- I'm standing for election for the Back to Basics Political Party and these are my fundamental beliefs ...
- There are too many people in our community who do not read for pleasure or self improvement and who, in fact, do not possess any books at all. This is how I would like you to help ...

Use these starters and speak in the style of a cool, calm, and collected speaker:

- It is completely possible, in fact environmentally essential, that we reduce our usage of toilet paper by 50 percent. This is how it can be done . . .
- It would make much more financial sense if all children were to delay starting school for a year. This is how it would work . . .

(CR) "Think left and think right and think low and think high. Oh, the thinks you can think up if only you try!" *Theodor Geisel (Dr. Seuss), author*

Use these starters and speak in the style of an energetic, lively, and passionate speaker:

- I have a plan that will entice all media celebrities to willingly donate 10 percent of their income to the Community Creativity Cause. It will be so appealing that celebrities will be clamoring to donate. Listen while I explain.
- I urge everyone to book a place on the weekend course I have just attended. It has changed my life in ways I can't describe. It's called "Think, Eat, and Breathe to Eternity" and this is how it can help you . . .

Use these starters and speak in the style of a humorous and light-hearted speaker:

- There are many ways to kiss the person you love, but this is a novel and fun way that is sure to make your partner go weak at the knees . . .
- Here is a surefire way to make you look busy and productive at work when in fact you can be as lazy as you like . . .

(PS) "There is no such thing as a problem without a gift for you in its hands. You seek problems because you need their gifts." *Richard Bach, author*

... In the World

- The most boring type of cookie in the world is ...
- The most irritating comedian in the world is ...
- The most ridiculous pet name in the world is ...
- The silliest newspaper article I've read in the world is ...
- The luckiest person in the world is ...

(CO) "Men are capable of talking hours on end over only one subject; women do it and don't even require a subject." *Curt Goetz, film actor*

- The worst TV advert in the world is ...
- The most useful words of wisdom in the world are ...
- The best place in the world to buy a takeaway is ...
- The greatest "how to" book in the world is ...
- The most impressive cover-up in the world was ...

(TD) "My darling girl, when are you going to understand that 'normal' isn't a virtue? It rather denotes a lack of courage." *Stockard Channing, actress*

Interviews

What would you ask these people or characters if you were to interview them?

- Mahatma Ghandi
- Salvador Dali
- Leonardo da Vinci

- John Wilkes Booth, assassinator of President Abraham Lincoln
- Lady Gaga

(CR) "Be daring, be different, be impractical, be anything that will assert integrity of purpose and imaginative vision against the play-it-safers, the creatures of the commonplace, the slaves of the ordinary." *Cecil Beaton, photographer*

- Harry Potter
- Robinson Crusoe
- Billy the Kid
- Homer Simpson
- Gandalf, from *The Lord of the Rings*

(PS) "It is well known that 'problem avoidance' is an important part of problem solving. Instead of solving the problem you go upstream and alter the system so that the problem does not occur in the first place." *Edward de Bono, physician*

Inventions and Innovations

- Can you think up a new kind of washing machine that works on a different principle than current ones?
- Can you design a new type of drinking glass that doesn't leave a mark on wooden tables?
- Can you think up three new and unusual flavors of potato chips?
- Can you devise a new concept for a board game? What is the general principle and what would the board and pieces look like?
- Most school photos have the class of students sitting or standing together facing the camera. What's a new and interesting way to capture a class of students?

(CO) "I always have a quotation for everything—it saves original thinking."
Dorothy L. Sayers, author

- In general, the world's population eats food by using knives, forks, and spoons, or chopsticks, or by using their hands. Devise new eating implements or a new way to consume food.
- Sometimes people throw or give away clothes, simply because they are no longer in fashion. Is there a way to avoid doing this?
- Vast amounts of aluminium cans are produced every year. What's a suitable alternative?
- When looking at the issue of drying clothes, could there be an alternative to hanging washing on the line or using a dryer?
- Libraries and book shops display books in the same way—on shelves. What's another way to display them?

(TD) "Put all your eggs in one basket and watch that basket." *Mark Twain, author*

Judging a Book by Its Title

Simply going on the title alone, why would people want to read a book called:

- I don't want to live on the edge; I want to live in the middle.
- I love myself more than I love anyone else.
- How to meet extremely successful people.
- How to eat easily and healthily on $1 a day.
- How to be lazy and get other people to do things for you.

> **(CR)** "Creativity represents a miraculous coming together of the uninhibited energy of the child with its apparent opposite and enemy, the sense of order imposed on the disciplined adult intelligence." *Norman Podhoretz, pundit*

- The five things you need to know to become a world-famous musician.
- Never have a job again: The better way to make a living.
- Why being bored is the best thing that could happen to you.
- You can become a millionaire by making craft items at home.
- Your other family: How to have close connections with your spirit guides and angels.

(PS) "It is wise to direct your anger towards problems—not people; to focus your energies on answers—not excuses." *William Arthur Ward, author*

Language

- What is the difference between written language and spoken language? Can you give an example?
- What is the maximum number of languages a human could learn?
- An eponym is a name or noun formed after a person. For example, July was named after Julius Caesar and Constantinople was named after the emperor Constantine. If you could have something named after you, what would it be and what would the new word be?
- We gain the meaning of something via its context. What is going on with the following three sentences, and why does English work like this?

o   The girl hit the boy with a hat.
o   I'm having my mom for lunch.
o   They gave her dog food.

- New words can bring richness to a language. The following sentence contains three invented words. What could the sentence mean? "She put on her schnoozak, made arrangements to wirringle with her friend, and drove to the mall callutively."

(CO) "The weakest punches are thrown with the tongue." *Robert Sharenow, author, television producer*

- Are there items or concepts without names that would benefit from being named?
- Would it be possible to change the English language so that it has phonetic spelling?
- What would people living fifty years ago have thought the meaning of the following words were:

    o   flash mob
    o   blog
    o   3D printer
    o   TweetDeck
    o   dad dancing
    o   FAQ
    o   search engine optimization
    o   ringtone
    o   spyware
    o   drama queen

- If a child had no human interaction from birth until seven years old and was left in a room with a TV playing, would they acquire language?

- In the nonsense poem "Jabberwocky" by Lewis Carroll, we can tell which words are the nouns, verbs, and so on, despite not recognizing or understanding what the words mean. How is this?

  'Twas brillig, and the slithy toves Did gyre and gimble in the wabe: All mimsy were the borogoves, And the mome raths outgrabe.

(TD) "There is a better way to do it—find it." *Thomas Edison, inventor*

Life Would Be Fun If . . .

- Life would be fun if we went back to the days of communicating with tom toms and smoke signals, right?
- Life would be fun if you and I had the powers of a superhero, right?
- Life would be fun if we didn't have to go to work on Mondays, right?
- Life would be fun if we could wear any old clothes and still look fabulous, right?
- Life would be fun if we went back to the days of black and white TV, right?

(CR) "Don't worry about people stealing an idea. If it's original, you'll have to ram it down their throats." *Howard Aiken, scientist*

- Life would be fun if eating chocolate and cream cakes helped you lose weight, right?
- Life would be fun if all the people who got on your nerves had an "off" button you could use whenever you liked, right?

- Life would be fun if it was a good thing to procrastinate, right?
- Life would be fun if the feeling of being in love lasted forever, right?
- Life would be fun if we went back to the days of having a tin bath in front of a fire, right?

(PS) "The only difference between a problem and a solution is that people understand the solution." *Charles Kettering, inventor*

Marriage

- The traditional wedding ceremony needs a revamp. How would you make it more You Tube friendly?
- Your husband, wife, or partner is getting on your nerves. Write an advert to sell them on an online auction site.
- Traditional marriage vows include the phrase *"for better, for worse."* Really? People want to stay together when it gets worse?
- Why are there romantic novels about "confirmed bachelors" who women want to marry? Why don't women just leave them alone and look for someone who is interested in commitment?
- Which would work better—an older man marrying a young woman or an older woman marrying a young man?

(CO) "Don't knock the weather; nine-tenths of the people couldn't start a conversation if it didn't change once in a while." *Kin Hubbard, cartoonist*

- Traditional western marriage vows may run along the lines of *"I, _____, take you, _____, to be my lawfully wedded (husband/wife), to have and to hold, from this day forward, for better, for worse, for richer, for poorer, in sickness and in health, until death do us part."* Given that statistics show that the average length of a marriage is around ten years, what changes would you make to the vows to make them fit the trend for shorter marriages?
- Pre-nuptial and post-nuptial agreements are old hat! A better way to deal with this is . . .
- Some people prefer not to marry another human being and instead marry an animal, a video game character, or even a pillow. Think of something else that people could marry and explain the benefits.
- Some African chiefs have over seventy wives. Firstly, why would someone want that many, and secondly how would they manage it all?
- Is there anyone who lives "happily ever after"?

(TD) "What luck for rulers, that men do not think." *Adolph Hitler*

Men and Women

- For women: If I were a man for a day, this is the advice I would give to women.
- If there were no difference between the type of clothes men and women wore, what effect would this have?
- It is a fact that men are better at . . .
- For women: If I were a man for a day, this is the advice I would give to other men.
- Katharine Hepburn said, "Sometimes I wonder if men and women really suit each other. Perhaps they should live next door and just visit now and then." Agree?

(CO) "When a woman says 'WHAT?' it's not because she didn't hear you. She's giving you a chance to change what you said." *Author unknown*

- It is a fact that women are better at ...
- For men: If I were a woman for a day, this is the advice I would give to men.
- If men's great achievements include painting the *Mona Lisa*, developing vaccines, inventing the steam engine, climbing Mount Everest, running a four-minute mile, and creating the theory of relativity, what are women's great achievements?
- John Gray wrote a book called *Men Are from Mars, Women Are from Venus*. Mars and Venus are only two planets apart. Are we really that similar?
- For men: If I were a woman for a day, this is the advice I would give to other women.

(CO) "When a woman is talking to you, listen to what she says with her eyes." *Victor Hugo, poet*

Minimalism

- You have decided to de-clutter. What is the *very first* thing you would get rid of?
- Could you throw away all of your printed photos?
- What would be the absolute minimum of items you could manage with in your kitchen?
- If you had to choose a maximum of five items of footwear and twenty-five items of clothing to live with, could you do it?
- Dealing with our possessions takes up a lot of time. How would people be more productive if they had fewer possessions?

> **(CR)** "An essential aspect of creativity is not being afraid to fail." *Edwin Land, scientist*

- What kind of person could never be a minimalist?
- It's said that "More isn't better; better is better." What does "better" mean?
- Do we really need to bother with having names? Would an individual identifier such as 31QSK be simpler?
- Is minimalism at odds with the culture of advertising?
- Are children in first-world countries with all the latest gadgets happier and better off than children in developing countries who have few possessions?

> **(TD)** "At a certain age some people's minds close up; they live on their intellectual fat." *William Lyon Phelps, author*

Mixed Bag

- If you had to choose only four photos that would give an overview of your life so far, which would you choose?
- You are invited to live in a remote village for a month with a tribe who elects a new chief every full moon. The tribe is primitive and lives very basically, but has enough housing, food, social interaction, and rudimentary education for the children. The new chief decides on an action that will help the village for the coming month. This time it's your turn to be chief. What action would you choose?
- Can you devise an unusual vacation that would suit people looking for adventure?
- Imagine that famous people had to work as gas station attendants for a month. Choose a famous person and say how you think they would cope.
- What's the difference between "quirky" and "weird"?

> **(CR)** "Creativity requires the courage to let go of certainties." *Erich Fromm, psychologist*

- Sumo wrestlers train hard and only eat two meals a day. Why are they so big?
- There is a religious sect of a Pacific island tribe who believes that Prince Philip, husband of Queen Elizabeth II, is a divine being, the pale-skinned son of a mountain spirit. If you had to devise a new religion based on a person, famous or otherwise, which person would you choose and what would the religion be?
- If New York City taxicabs were to be painted pink instead of yellow, what would be the consequences?
- What would cars look like if people had long bodies, short arms, and short legs?
- If the story of Noah's Ark is true, how did Noah manage to stop the carnivores from eating other animals, and how did he feed them?

(PS) "Most of my advances were by mistake. You uncover what is when you get rid of what isn't." *R. Buckminster Fuller, architect*

Money

- If we were to live without money for a day and had to barter instead, what would you use to barter with?
- Imagine that in a minute's time, three unknown people come into the room. You all sit around a table, place whatever cash and banknotes you have with you onto the table, then divide it out equally. Would you do it?
- If you could take $100 and go back in time one hundred years, how would you spend it?
- You buy a new house and find a sack full of old banknotes that are no longer legal tender. What would you do?

- Your quirky great aunt has died, and in her will she has left you a large sum of money on condition that you spend every Saturday for a year dressed as a chicken, going door to door collecting money for the animal sanctuary that re-houses ex-battery hens. Would you do it?

(PS) "Start where you are. Use what you have. Do what you can."
Arthur Ashe, tennis player

- Under what conditions could you—literally—burn money?
- If, like Robin Hood, you were to rob from the rich and give to the poor, would it make any difference? Would the poor know how to look after the money?
- Is it possible to have one world-wide currency?
- Instead of paying taxes, we should . . .
- Coins, banknotes, and cards are so outdated! Instead it would be better to use . . .

(TD) "Thoughts, like fleas, jump from man to man. But they don't bite everybody." *Stanislaw Lec, poet*

Music

- Think of the most ridiculous tune you know. Who does it remind you of?
- If you were stuck in an elevator that was playing the same song over and over, how many times do you think you could hear it before starting to go mad?
- What is the worst musical instrument when it comes to listening to a beginner practicing?
- What kind of music would be suitable for a stage production titled "Dracula meets Mickey Mouse and Calamity Jane"?
- What kind of music do you think elephants would like?

(CR) "The chief enemy of creativity is 'good' sense." *Pablo Picasso, painter*

- Does it take real talent to be able to sing every note out of tune?
- As there are so many songs with lyrics about love, why don't we all love one another?
- Tell us about someone who has real bad taste in music.
- Why do people rarely write song lyrics about things like architecture, engineering, and international banking?

(PS) "A problem, to be a problem, must contain an unknown. If all was known, the problem would vanish." *Alan C. Walter, founder of Knowledgism*

Name Something or Someone

- Name something that starts with the letter A that you have avoided on purpose.
- Name something that starts with the letter S that will always make you laugh.
- Name something that starts with the letter L that scares you.
- Name something that starts with the letter T that makes you roll your eyes.
- Name something that starts with the letter P that you would pay a lot of money for.

(CO) "Do not put your cleverness in front of the communication." *Paul Arden, author*

- Name someone whose name starts with the letter F you've been envious of.
- Name someone whose name starts with the letter C who is either grumpier or happier than you.
- Name someone whose name starts with the letter J that you would give your last candy to.

- Name someone whose name starts with the letter M who you wouldn't want to sit next to on a long bus journey.
- Name someone whose name starts with the letter D who is the last person you would ever marry.

(TD) "All great thinkers are initially ridiculed—and eventually revered." *Robin S. Sharma, author, thinker on leadership, personal growth, and life management*

Neighbors .

- There are two almost identical houses for sale on a street, either of which you would like to live in. One of the houses has neighbors who run a karaoke bar and like to have lots of friends around to use one of their karaoke machines in the garden. The other has neighbors who keep owls that make loud, scary, screeching noises at night time. If you had to choose one of the houses, which would you choose?
- You have new neighbors. They come round to ask if you would like to have an underground bunker built between your houses, with access from both, in case of a nuclear disaster. What would you say?
- You are at a party and overhear one of your neighbors describing you as "quirky, creative, great fun, and eccentric." What would you think?
- You move into a new house where your neighbors are the longest standing residents on the street. They come round to see you with a piece of paper on which they have written down all the aspects they dislike about people on the street: The husband at number 17 swears too much; the children at number

9 have no manners; the family at number 12 don't clean their toilet; and so on. What would you do?

- Think of all the people in the neighborhood you know. Who would you go to if you needed to borrow some sugar? Who would you go to if you wanted help carrying something heavy? Who would you go to if you wanted them to sign a Save the Whales petition?

(CR) "Creativity comes from a conflict of ideas." *Donatella Versace, designer*

- Your neighbor's fruit tree overhangs your garden. You've asked them politely to prune it, but they have chosen not to, so you take the fruit that is hanging on your side of the fence and use it. They get angry and say it's their fruit. What would you do?
- You are at a party and overhear one of your neighbors describing you as "intelligent, articulate, and an upstanding member of the community." What would you think?
- What's the most ridiculous neighbor dispute you've come across?
- You have decided to have a fancy dress street barbecue. Which neighbor would you ask to help you organize it, and what do you think the response from the other neighbors would be?
- New neighbors move in who do things at different times from the majority of people. They mow the lawn at midnight, repair the car or do DIY at five o'clock in the morning, and sit outside having conversations until the early hours. Would you say anything?

(PS) "It's not a problem that we have a problem. It's a problem if we don't deal with the problem." *Mary Kay Utecht, educator*

New Products

- Could you invent something that will mean you get a seat on a crowded bus or train every time?
- Some people take a long time to learn to drive. What new product could cut people's learning time in half?
- Eating spaghetti is difficult for some people. Formulate a device to make it easier.
- Devise something that would reduce the amount of time spent on washing the dishes but would leave them equally as clean.
- For men who don't want to shave every day but who want to look clean-shaven, what new product could help?

(TD) "The surest way to corrupt a youth is to instruct him to hold in higher esteem those who think alike than those who think differently." *Friedrich Nietzsche, philologist, philosopher, and composer*

- We could cut the time spent at college in half if people could learn twice as quickly. Devise a way to do this.
- What new product could help people with insomnia?
- Cell phones will eventually be replaced by what new product?
- What new product could put an end to having to clean the toilet?
- What could be invented to give us more control over the weather?

(CO) "I never learn anything talking. I only learn things when I ask questions." *Lou Holtz, football coach*

New Skills

You have been invited to learn a new skill. Which of the following would be most useful to learn?

- Bareback riding, fortune telling, or Mongolian cookery?
- How to cut your family's hair, how to grow olives, or how to make silk roses?
- How to ride a unicycle, how to spray paint a car, or how to do card tricks?
- How to speak Swahili, how to do henna painting on hands, or how to crochet a blanket?
- How to paint photorealism (a painting that appears to be photographic), how to fly a glider airplane, or how to groom a dog?

(CR) "It's not what you look at that matters, it's what you see." *Henry David Thoreau, author*

- The art of calligraphy, graphology (the study and analysis of handwriting), or wine tasting?
- How to build a dry stone wall, how to set up a neighborhood watch group, or how to handle a firearm?
- How to be a catwalk model, how to juggle, or defensive driving?
- How to swim backstroke, how to bind a hardback book, or taxidermy?
- How to build a computer from scratch, how to tie a bow tie, or how to brew beer?

(PS) "For every complex problem there is an answer that is clear, simple, and wrong." *H. L. Mencken, journalist*

New Year

- Tell us about the most unusual New Year's Eve celebration you have held or attended.

- What's the point of making a New Year's resolution? Don't most people give up on them by January 3?
- What's a better way to start the year than making a new year's resolution?
- What difference would it make to a person's life if they were born on the first day of the year, instead of a day earlier on the last day of the year?
- How would life be different if we thought in half years rather than full years?

> **(CO)** "A good conversation always involves a certain amount of complaining. I like to bond over mutual hatreds and petty grievances." *Lisa Kleypas, author*

- Why do different cultures have their new year at different times? For example, the Chinese New Year's date falls between January 21 and February 21 depending on when the new moon of the first lunar month falls; the Jewish New Year is celebrated in autumn on the first two days of the seventh month of the Hebrew calendar; the Islamic New Year falls on the first day of Muharram, which is the first month in the Islamic calendar; the Thai New Year is celebrated from April 13–15; and the Ethiopian New Year is usually on September 11.
- If Christmas Island/Kiribati and Samoa reach the New Year twenty-six hours before Baker Island and Howland Island in the US, what difference does this make?
- All racehorses in the northern hemisphere celebrate their official birthday on January 1. What would happen if people did this, too?
- Why do we split time into periods of a year?

- Why do we have other new years within the main year, for example, the start of the financial year or the start of the academic year? Why don't they all start at the same time?

(TD) "Did you ever stop to think, and forget to start again?" *Winnie the Pooh, fictional bear*

Nothing

- Is there such a thing as "nothing"?
- Your friend calls you up saying they have a gift for you. You arrange a time for them to come around, and wait in anticipation. They give you a gift-wrapped box about 12" by 12" by 12", but when you open it, it is empty. What could be a valid reason that someone would give you nothing?
- If you were to spend the day doing "nothing," what would you actually do?
- What is the longest amount of time you could manage to buy nothing at all?
- If you were in a closed, windowless room without any light source at all, would you be able to see "nothing"?

(CR) "You don't have to be creative to be creative." *Paul Arden, author*

- Is "not anything" the same as "nothing"?
- If someone said they knew "nothing" about a particular topic, while someone else said they knew "everything" about it, could they both be correct?

- If someone has a new idea and creates an innovative and unique product that is unlike any other, will the idea have come from nothing?
- If a woman looks upset, and her husband asks her what is wrong and she replies "nothing," what does she actually mean?
- What does it mean, literally, when people say they will "stop at nothing" to get something they want?

(PS) "Our tendency to create heroes rarely jibes with the reality that most nontrivial problems require collective solutions." *Warren Bennis, author*

Odd One Out

There are four words listed, and while there may be no obvious link among any of them, see how many ways you can find to deem one of them as the odd one out. There are no right or wrong answers.

- TONSILS – CHEETAH – LOGICAL – LUCK
- BARTENDER – MUSTARD – JEALOUSY – SUNSHINE
- NEPHEW – MOTORBIKE – CAVIAR – UNDERHAND
- SPECIAL – THOROUGH – IMAGINATION – NOSE
- SAGITTARIUS – LOOFAH – MAGICIAN – SMELLY

(CO) "The trouble with talking too fast is you may say something you haven't thought of yet." *Ann Landers, columnist*

- CAMERA – LONGITUDE – SHIRT – SUNFLOWER
- PRESIDENT – CAULIFLOWER – TORNADO – MONSTER
- TEAM – SAND – THINK – CAMOUFLAGE
- CHERRY – HOVERCRAFT – SPANIEL – THIRSTY
- LIBRARY – ROWING – CONCERT – ANTARCTICA

(TD) "People should think things out fresh and not just accept conventional terms and the conventional way of doing things." *R. Buckminster Fuller, architect*

Older People

- When you were younger, what age seemed "old"? Now what age seems old?
- You've been asked to "babysit" someone's grumpy grandfather for a day and you decide to take a box of items to see if it will keep him interested. What would you take?
- What could you recommend to a group of women in their sixties and seventies to avoid the "mutton dressed as lamb" look?
- Give some humorous advice to older people about being old!
- Imagine you are with a group of your younger family members and had to give each one a piece of advice starting with, "When I was your age . . ." What would you say?

(CR) "Don't have good ideas if you aren't willing to be responsible for them." *Alan J. Perlis, computer scientist*

- When does old age begin?
- Who is an example of what *not* to do when you get old?
- If people in their seventies were to train teenagers in how to look stylish the way they did when they were a teenager, what would they say?

- Describe two people of the same age, one of whom looks significantly older than the other. What's caused the difference?
- Is it OK for older people to dress in teenage clothes?

(PS) "Leaders think and talk about the solutions. Followers think and talk about the problems." *Brian Tracy, author*

One Hundred Years

- What changes would a one-hundred-year-old person have noticed regarding food shopping?
- In one hundred years from now what will have happened to the fast food industry?
- If you took one hundred regular people and placed them on a remote island without any form of communication with the outside world, built a wall down the middle, and placed half of the people on one side and half on the other, after one hundred years what differences would there be in the two groups?
- What changes would a one-hundred-year-old person have noticed regarding underwear?
- In one hundred years from now what will have happened to the ways to correct eyesight problems?

(CO) "When people talk, listen completely. Most people never listen." *Ernest Hemingway, author*

- Why would a judge impose a jail sentence of one hundred years?
- What changes would a one-hundred-year-old person have noticed regarding marriage and relationships?

- Give an overview of one hundred years' worth of piano sheet music.
- In one hundred years from now what will have happened to the Bollywood movie industry?
- If the world is already advancing at a rapid pace, how much faster can things change in the next one hundred years?

(TD) "The thoughts that come often unsought, and, as it were, drop into the mind, are commonly the most valuable of any we have." *John Locke, philosopher*

Only One

If there could be only one of the following in the world, which would it have to be and why?

- Language
- Non-alcoholic beverage other than water
- Form of government
- Type of pet
- Religion

(CR) "I remembered a story of how Bach was approached by a young admirer one day and asked, 'But Papa Bach, how do you manage to think of all these new tunes?' 'My dear fellow,' Bach is said to have answered, according to my version, 'I have no need to think of them. I have the greatest difficulty not to step on them when I get out of bed in the morning and start moving around my room.'" *Laurens Van Der Post, author*

- Hairstyle for women
- Type of car
- Type of footwear
- Form of heating
- Sport

(PS) "Any problem, big or small, within a family, always seems to start with bad communication. Someone isn't listening." *Emma Thompson, actress*

Ordinary Situations

How could you take an ordinary situation and make it different, interesting, unusual, or even extraordinary?

- Each week you meet with a couple of friends after work in a bar in town. You always meet in the same bar and have a drink and chat for an hour or two.
- From Monday to Friday when you get home from work, your partner has made the evening meal and you sit down at the dining table with the family. The meal takes thirty to forty minutes.
- For many years you have been going to the same hairdresser every six weeks and having the same hairstyle.
- Your morning routine comprises getting up at 7 a.m., having a shower, getting dressed, eating breakfast, making the bed, then leaving for work at 8 a.m.
- In January you always plan your summer vacation. You take the same two weeks in July and go to a similar resort within your country.

(CO) "It was impossible to get a conversation going, everybody was talking too much." *Yogi Berra, baseball manager*

- Once a fortnight on a Saturday morning you go to the library and choose a fiction book by similar authors, which you read for about an hour in bed several nights a week.

- You pick up your children from school, bring them home, give them an afternoon snack, then let them watch TV for an hour.
- Once a week on a Thursday evening you go to the supermarket to buy a week's worth of food. You go the same way round the supermarket aisles and buy the same type of food.
- Every year on your partner's birthday, you wait until they get home from work to open their presents, then you go out for a meal.
- You phone your parents every week on a Sunday evening and chat for about half an hour about what you have all been doing.

> **(TD)** "It's easy to come up with new ideas; the hard part is letting go of what worked for you two years ago, but will soon be out of date." *Roger von Oech, speaker*

People and Situations

How would these people react in these situations?

- An old Italian villager at a New York disco
- An elite athlete at his son's school egg and spoon race
- A prim and proper English Lady in a mixed sauna
- A teenager from The Bronx at a yoga class
- A snobbish MasterChef at a fast food outlet

> **(CR)** "The creative person is both more primitive and more cultivated, more destructive, a lot madder and a lot saner, than the average person." *Frank Barron, baseball player*

- A Christian nun at a video game convention
- A famous pop star at a scout camp
- A pacifist at a commando course
- A newly and happily married couple at a divorce seminar
- An eighty-year-old woman at a lingerie party

(PS) "Ah, mastery . . . what a profoundly satisfying feeling when one finally gets on top of a new set of skills . . . and then sees the light under the new door those skills can open, even as another door is closing." *Gail Sheehy, author*

Pets and Animals

- If you were going to introduce an educational school classroom for dogs, what would they learn?
- Imagine you are Noah and that the flood is about to happen. Your Ark is very small and you can only fit six species of animal on it. Which would you choose?
- Which animal most closely resembles you in looks, personality, or behavior?
- The three types of pet I would keep if I lived in a lighthouse are . . .
- Cat and dog lovers could widen their views. There are many more interesting pets to have and ways to look after them. For example . . .

(CO) "Most of the successful people I've known are the ones who do more listening than talking." *Bernard Baruch, financier*

- If there was a Bring Your Pet to Work Day, what arrangements would have to be made?
- If animals could speak to humans ...
- Is it OK to dye your pet, give them a Mohican hair style, or put them in a Yoda fancy dress outfit?
- Why do pandas look so cute?
- Why is Santa's sleigh pulled by flying reindeer?

(TD) "Opinion is that exercise of the human will which helps us to make a decision without information." *John Erskine, educator*

Photography

- Tell us about the worst school photo you have seen.
- Tell us about the worst wedding photo you have seen.
- If there were three versions of a head and shoulders photo—one in sepia, one in black and white, and one in color—what would be the different messages each one gave?
- You've been asked to photograph a knife and fork so that they look "happening." How would you do it?
- What photo could you create to illustrate the concept of "forgetfulness"?

(CR) "Sometimes I've believed as many as six impossible things before breakfast." *Lewis Carroll, author*

- The big picture or the little picture: Which would work better, a landscape photo of a beautiful building in a magnificent setting or several close-up photos showing the intricacies of the external architecture?

- You've been asked to photograph a bicycle so that it looks "exotic." How would you do it?
- How could you make a photograph of people in 1980s clothing look more modern?
- You've been asked to photograph a geometry set so that it looks "cute." How would you do it?
- What photo could you create to illustrate the concept of "integrity"?

(PS) "To solve any problem, here are three questions to ask yourself: First, what could I do? Second, what could I read? And third, who could I ask?" *Jim Rohn, author*

Physical Appearance

- If you could look like a famous person for a day, who would you look like?
- If you changed gender, what kind of clothes and shoes would you wear, and what hairstyle would you have?
- Forget colored hair dye, funky clothes, and tattoos! Here's a much better way to exhibit your identity to the world . . .
- What can you suggest that would make having gray hair appear fashionable?
- What would make a good alternative to expensive skin tanning products?

(CO) "Take care of speaking thoughtlessly; when a man's heart is upset, words travel faster than wind and rain." *Amenemope, pharaoh*

- People who look androgynous have neither a clearly masculine nor clearly feminine appearance. If you had to change three of your features to make yourself look androgynous, what would you change?

- Rod Stewart's song title claims, "Blondes have more fun." Do they?
- Why does hair go gray when we get older?
- What would happen if once people reached the age of eighteen they didn't look any older for the rest of their lives?
- What would happen if "man boobs" became trendy?

(PS) "Don't dwell on what went wrong. Instead, focus on what to do next. Spend your energies on moving forward toward finding the answer." *Denis Waitley, author*

Post-nominal Letters

Post-nominal letters are letters placed after a person's name to show the position, educational degree, accreditation, office, or honor that a person holds. Work out what these fictional post-nominal letters could stand for and what someone would need to do in order to achieve them:

- J. Smith CHFW
- J. Smith Dipl. CCT
- J. Smith P. Nod
- J. Smith EIEIO
- J. Smith M Frs. Hons

(CR) "Creative people are curious, flexible, persistent, and independent with a tremendous spirit of adventure and a love of play." *Henri Matisse, artist*

- J. Smith SANOO
- J. Smith TC-An
- J. Smith QWWI

- J. Smith L. Ph
- J. Smith SSE-T

(TD) "But don't be satisfied with stories, how things have gone with others. Unfold your own myth, without complicated explanation." *Rumi, poet*

Quotes

Do you agree with these quotes?

- "The difference between stupidity and genius is that genius has its limits." Albert Einstein, physicist
- "A creative man is motivated by the desire to achieve, not by the desire to beat others." Ayn Rand, novelist
- "Quirky is what a guy would call a girl he doesn't understand." Kat Dennings, actress
- "A joke is a very serious thing." Winston Churchill, British prime minister
- "Men are allowed to age. Men are allowed to gain weight. Men are allowed to be quirky looking." Janeane Garofalo, comedian

(CO) "A single conversation across the table with a wise man is better than ten years mere study of books." *Henry Wadsworth Longfellow, poet*

- "Almost always, the creative dedicated minority has made the world better." Martin Luther King Jr., civil rights activist
- "In prehistoric times, mankind often had only two choices in crisis situations: fight or flee. In modern times, humor offers us a third alternative; fight, flee—or laugh." Robert Orben, author

- "Bad, quirky poetry might be better than some of the good stuff, because it really comes from the heart." Cheryl Hines, actress
- "Fascinatingly confident, rude people are great." Steven Moffat, television writer
- "Start every day off with a smile and get it over with." W. C. Fields, comedian

---

(TD) "Reserve your right to think, for even to think wrongly is better than not to think at all." *Hypatia, philosopher*

Relationships and Romance

- You are in a new romance and want to make sure the person is right for you. What five pertinent questions could you ask to check if they are suitable?
- Would you give a high five at the end of your first date?
- Can you state three of the ways you are the perfect partner to have when it comes to relationships?
- When was the last time you felt weak at the knees over someone?
- What public displays of affection make you go "Ewwww"?

(CR) "Creativity comes from looking for the unexpected and stepping outside your own experience." *Masaru Ibuka, co-founder of Sony*

- The man of your dreams has turned into a couch potato. Is it time to trade him in for a better model?
- If you were to read the first and last paragraphs of a romantic novel, do you think you could work out the gist of the story?

- Why do some people refer to their partner as their "better half"?
- What's the point of being attentive to your boyfriend or girlfriend in the beginning when it's all going to change later?
- Why do some women want to be whisked off by a knight in shining armor?

(PS) "If you can talk brilliantly about a problem, it can create the consoling illusion that it has been mastered." *Stanley Kubrick, film director*

Semantic Fields

We store all the words we know, not in any random fashion in our head, but in groups of similar words called semantic fields. For example, we may store the words laughing, giggling, chuckling, and sniggering in the same semantic field.

- Think of as many words as you can in the same semantic field as the word "creative."
- Think of as many words as you can in the same semantic field as the word "problem."
- Think of as many words as you can in the same semantic field as the word "quirky."
- Think of as many words as you can in the same semantic field as the word "conversation."
- Think of as many words as you can in the same semantic field as the word "thinking."

(CO) "If you ever have to support a flagging conversation, introduce the topic of eating." *Leigh Hunt, poet*

How many words you can come up with that are not in the same semantic field, nor are opposites or antonyms, and have no relation at all to the word given?

- Think of as many words as you can that have no relation to the word "innovation."
- Think of as many words as you can that have no relation to the word "language."
- Think of as many words as you can that have no relation to the word "dance."
- Think of as many words as you can that have no relation to the word "music."
- Think of as many words as you can that have no relation to the word "art."

(TD) "What a blessing it is to be alone with your thoughts when so many are alone with their inability to think." *Robert Brault, author*

Stand in a Line

You have been asked to join nine people who are standing in a line based on where they fall on a continuum of 1–10. For example, if the continuum were for "risk taking," at position 1 would be someone who never takes risks, and at position 10 would be someone who takes many and large risks. Which position would you place yourself at:

- For wearing fashionable clothes?
- For being able to bake a cake?
- For being afraid of ghosts?
- For being good at choosing gifts for others?
- For being able to find a bargain?

(CR) "Do not fear to be eccentric in opinion, for every opinion now accepted was once eccentric." *Bertrand Russell, philosopher*

- For having an interesting name?
- For having nice knuckles?
- For being able to name all the US states?
- For remembering to put the garbage out?
- For being able to answer quirky questions?

(PS) "Some problems are so complex that you have to be highly intelligent and well-informed just to be undecided about them."
Laurence J. Peter, educator

Stories with Messages

Think of or make up a story or anecdote that gives the message:

- Too many cooks spoil the broth.
- Humility.
- Not taking yourself too seriously.
- Abundance.
- A journey of a thousand miles begins with a single step.

(CO) "If writers wrote as carelessly as some people talk, then adhasdh asdglaseuyt[bn[pasdlgkhasdfasdf." *Lemony Snicket, novelist*

- Laughter is the best medicine.
- Creativity.
- Dig the well before you need the water.
- Endurance.
- You have to kiss a lot of frogs before you find your handsome prince.

(TD) "Too often we enjoy the comfort of opinion without the discomfort of thought." *John F. Kennedy, former US president*

Tall Tales

Using the following story starters, begin telling a tall tale (a story with unbelievable elements, related as if it were true and factual). After a short while the next person carries on with the story, and the next, until all people have had a go:

- Jordan looked in the spare room and got the surprise of his life ...
- Rachel took her shoes off and stood in the bucket of washing-up water as instructed ...
- Kira called me up yelling, "Only three more to go!" ...
- "Oh my goodness!" shouted Gillian, "I think my mother has taken the dog's tablets" ...
- Never in the history of mankind had this happened before ...

(CR) "I just invent, then wait until man comes around to needing what I've invented." *R. Buckminster Fuller, architect*

- "It was horrible!" shuddered Mark, "all blue and lumpy" ...
- It came silently. So quietly that no one was aware of its presence ...
- It started off as a normal Sunday afternoon drive ...
- "Things would be OK," sighed Phil, "if only he would stop thinking that we are living in the 1960s" ...
- "I'm sorry," apologized Joy, "but I've spent a month's salary on ..."

(PS) "No problem can be solved from the same level of consciousness that created it." *Albert Einstein, physicist*

The Body

- What would happen if we could go into a meditative state for three days?
- How would things be different if everyone lived until they were exactly seventy-five years old?
- If the way to produce offspring was not via sexual reproduction and babies really were delivered by storks, what difference would this make to society's behavior?
- If we could sleep standing up ...
- If our bodies were made of something similar to modelling clay and we could shape it as we liked, what would your body look like?

(CO) "It is all right to hold a conversation but you should let go of it now and then." *Richard Armour, poet*

- If men, not women, gave birth, how would the world be different?
- If bodies had been designed so that our hearing came via our feet not our ears, how would humankind have adapted?
- Is there a body shape that looks "intelligent"?
- If the man-made physical environment were designed for older people with mobility issues, how would it be different?
- Why are our nose and mouth so close together when they are the only ways we can breathe? Would it be better to have them in different parts of the body?

(TD) "Who so would be a man must also be a non-conformist." *Ralph Waldo Emerson, essayist*

Think Think Think

- How could "thinking small" be the best solution to an issue?
- If you were to stop doing things for the purpose of making people like you, what would you be capable of doing?
- Why does society generally place technological development above spiritual development?
- What is the purpose of an ego? Are we using ours to its true potential?
- Think of something yet to be achieved—small or large—and explain how someone could achieve the unachievable.

(CR) "Nothing encourages creativity like the chance to fall flat on one's face." *James D. Finley, executive*

- Is it better to have a bad idea and go in the wrong direction or not have any ideas and stay where you are?
- Failure can be a great teacher if we learn from its lessons. Describe one of your most spectacular failures and say what you learned from it.
- What is the conventional point of view about education followed by a career? And what is a more interesting, non-conventional point of view?
- Why do most people aim for mediocrity?

- What is the merit in starting a project before you have perfected everything, and then fixing it as you go?

(PS) "The single biggest problem in communication is the illusion that it has taken place." *George Bernard Shaw, playwright*

This and That

- You have a blank piece of paper. What could you draw or write on it that would capture your essence as a creative person?
- What's "alternative" about alternative medicine?
- What are uninspiring people like?
- Why is it that there is too much of one thing in some places in the world (sunshine, water, food, crops, money, possessions, housing, etc.) and not enough in others?
- Why are people fascinated by the Leaning Tower of Pisa? It's only leaning!

(CO) "In conversation avoid the extremes of forwardness and reserve." *John Byrom, poet*

- Nine a.m. on Monday morning. What are all the mental images and emotions this phrase could produce?
- When is it a good idea to take "no" for an answer?
- Is it better to be a person who has too many new ideas or a person who never has any new ideas?
- Give one benefit for getting the worst mark in an exam.
- If you had to devise a five-hundred-year plan for the future of the world, where would you start?

(TD) "When you see a good move, look for a better one." *Emanuel Lasker, world chess champion*

Time and Speed

- Instead of spending six straight hours a day at school five days a week, the alternative is to . . .
- If days lasted twenty-five hours . . .
- If children could hold intelligible conversations at the age of twelve months . . .
- Should the legal driving speed be halved?
- If people only needed three hours' sleep a night . . .

(CR) "I never did very well in math—I could never seem to persuade the teacher that I hadn't meant my answers literally." *Calvin Trillin, journalist*

- If every business had to operate 24/7 . . .
- Would it be a good idea to raise the school leaving age to twenty?
- If humans could live to be 150 years old . . .
- To become an overnight success . . .
- If we could speak twice as fast as we do . . .

(PS) "It's so much easier to suggest solutions when you don't know too much about the problem." *Malcolm S. Forbes, publisher*

Time Travel

- You have a time machine and are planning to travel forward to the year 2500 with your family. What would you be most worried about?

- You have a time machine and are planning to travel backward to the year 100 with your family. What would you pack in your suitcase?
- You are writing the movie script for an eerie story about time travel. What would the movie be about?
- You have been given the opportunity to time travel just once in your life and you can only travel back in time, not forward. You can choose a day in your life and re-live those twenty-four hours. How and when would you use this opportunity?
- If you could go forward in time one week, would you find out the lottery results?

(CO) "Conversation between Adam and Eve must have been difficult at times because they had nobody to talk about." *Agnes Repplier, essayist*

- If you could go back in time and save a now-extinct species, would you?
- Some people think that aliens are not from other planets but are from another time. Agree?
- If you could go back in time and stop yourself from making a major mistake, what would you do?
- If you could go back in time to when the Pyramids were being built, what do you think you would see?
- Some people think that Leonardo da Vinci was a time traveler. What is the argument in favor of this?

(TD) "Had I not created my whole world, I would certainly have died in other people's." *Anaïs Nin, author*

TV

- Can you devise a new TV series suitable for quirky, creative people?
- Think up a great TV advert to sell frozen sprouts.
- If you could combine two TV programs, which two would you choose and what would the new program be like?
- Would you like to be able to watch TV twice as fast so you could see twice as many programs?
- Would you make a good TV chat show host?

(CR) "If at first, the idea is not absurd, then there is no hope for it." *Albert Einstein, physicist*

- How can we liven up the TV news programs?
- Which TV channel should be scrapped?
- Is it a good idea to have TV programs shown on buses and trains?
- What is the most boring TV program of all time?
- What would a home makeover program, made with the lowest budget possible, be like?

(PS) "The biggest problem in the world could have been solved when it was small." *Witter Bynner, poet*

Unusual Concepts

- It appears that most people think that leaving grass in its natural green color is a good idea. What if it became more acceptable to dye grass?

- It appears that most people in the Western world think that having all their head covered by hair—when possible—is a good idea. What if it became more acceptable to have 50 percent of their head covered by hair?
- It appears that most people think that having pictures and paintings on the walls is a good idea. What if it became more acceptable to have them on the ceiling?
- It appears that most people think that having your own house and furniture is a good idea. What if it became more acceptable to not own or rent a specific place or possess furniture, and to move house every so often, simply taking your personal items?
- It appears that most people think that traveling to places by the quickest method is a good idea. What if it became more acceptable to travel by the slowest method?

(CO) "The lower one speaks the closer a woman listens." *Marcel Achard, playwright*

- It appears that most people think that punishing people who commit crimes is a good idea. What if it became more acceptable to praise people who committed crimes?
- It appears that most people think that having military ranks in the armed forces is a good idea. What if people had no rank? How could it work?
- It appears that most people think that watching TV as a form of recreation is a good idea. What if it became more acceptable to only use it to watch educational programs?

- It appears that most people think that having books for the purpose of reading is a good idea. What if it became more acceptable to use books for a completely different purpose?
- It appears that most people think that having a cat flap to let the cat in and out of the house is a good idea. What if it became more acceptable to train cats to ring a front door bell?

(TD) "When it can't be done do it. If you don't do it, it doesn't exist." *Paul Arden, author*

Unusual Events

What unusual events could have led to someone genuinely saying:

- "...and that's why I ate only tomatoes for fourteen days."
- "...and he believed it was an alien in his bathroom."
- "...which is why she went on a search for the biggest kiwi fruit in the world."
- "...so my conclusion is that the majority of dinosaurs were purple."
- "...and I can't imagine ever wanting to drink pumpkin juice again."

(CR) "Creative minds have always been known to survive any kind of bad training." *Anna Freud, psychologist*

- "...it took me three years to complete a forty-piece jigsaw, but it was worth it."
- "...and that's how I learned to be an expert in toe wrestling."

- ". . . which is why I have to change my name to John Tchaikovsky Vivaldi Handel Bach Chopin Smith."
- ". . . but I wouldn't recommend anyone else goes deep sea diving wearing mountain climbing gear."
- ". . . and that's how my painting of a giraffe in a cowboy outfit came about."

(PS) " 'It depends' is almost always the right answer to any big question." *Linus Torvalds, software engineer*

What Can We Learn From . . .

We can take useful lessons from most things in life if we look deeply enough. What can we learn from . . .

- Mickey Mouse?
- Usain Bolt?
- Santa Claus?
- People who go on reality TV shows?
- Sherpa Tenzing?

(CR) "When patterns are broken, new worlds emerge." *Tuli Kupferberg, poet*

- Winnie the Pooh?
- Michael Jackson?
- People who have lots of tattoos and piercings?
- People who live alone in remote areas?
- Ourselves?

(TD) "Anyone can look for fashion in a boutique or history in a museum. The creative explorer looks for history in a hardware store and fashion in an airport." *Robert Wieder, journalist*

What Could Be the Benefits Of . . .

- Leaving your blinds and curtains closed all the time?
- Having dessert before the main course?
- Sleeping sideways across the bed?
- Giving a presentation while facing away from the audience?
- Wearing odd shoes?

(CR) "They are ill discoverers that think there is no land, when they can see nothing but sea." *Francis Bacon, English lord chancellor*

- Taking a job of a much lower status than you are used to?
- Speaking in a foreign accent for a day?
- Drinking coffee only on Wednesdays?
- Trying to decipher an ancient writing system that hasn't yet been deciphered?
- Hanging your washing on the line in alphabetical order?

(PS) "Again and again, the impossible decision is solved when we see that the problem is only a tough decision waiting to be made." *Dr. Robert Schuller, pastor*

What Would You Do If . . .

- You did a Google images search on "mutton dressed as lamb" and found a photo of yourself?

- You were going for a job interview, were almost there, had no time to spare, and the zip on your trousers broke?
- You left your personal diary on a train?
- You found out that your great grandfather, who was stationed in a small village overseas with the military, had married another woman there and you now have thirty relatives you weren't aware of?
- You were asked to go on stage during a magic performance and help with a trick that involved holding a six-foot snake?

(CO) "Conversation is an exercise of the mind; gossip is merely an exercise of the tongue." *Author unknown*

- One of your work colleagues claimed to be the rightful heir to the throne of Scotland and asked for your support?
- You were asked during a job interview, "Tell us the funniest joke you've ever heard"?
- You belong to a sports team with a strict dress code, where players wear green tops and green shorts. You are getting ready but can't find your green shorts. You only have red ones or white ones, and it's fifteen minutes till you need to be there.
- The book you want to buy is on special offer at a vastly discounted price of $10 for one hour only. Usually it is $80. You are on your own, have $5 cash and no cards with you, and there is ten minutes to go.
- The movie you want to see starts in ten minutes, there is only one showing of it, and you want to know exactly what happens at the beginning. You are still at home, the car is getting repaired, there is no one available to give you a lift, and arranging for a cab would take too

long to get you there in time. If you walk to the cinema it will take you twenty-five minutes.

(CR) "It is the eye of ignorance that assigns a fixed and unchangeable color to every object; beware of this stumbling block." *Paul Gauguin, artist*

Who Is This?

Below are descriptions of different personality types. Who do you know who most fits these descriptions, and does one of the characteristics perfectly describe them?

- Strong willed and determined, they will stop at nothing to achieve their goals. They don't believe in taking life easy and wasting any talents they have been given. They are bossy but fair.
- Pleasant and easy going, they will do anything for an easy life. Often at home reading or relaxing, they are good listeners and are very happy to give a lot of their time to other people.
- Unsettled and fractious, they do many things at the same time. They can't decide on one life path and are often pulled in several directions, doing none of them with any conviction. They are unable to relax or stay in the house much.
- Cheeky and funny, they are always pushing the boundaries. They like to bend rules and make life bigger and better. Very charismatic, they are attractive to members of the opposite sex.
- Peaceful, spiritual, and alternative. They rarely join in with traditional life, preferring to live on the margins and live life their own way. The concepts of social norms and social pressure are anathema to them.

(TD) "It is well for people who think, to change their minds occasionally in order to keep them clean." *Luther Burbank, botanist*

- Concerned about having a perfect house, they ensure all furniture and decorations match each other and are in impeccable condition. Not a thing is out of place and they worry that visitors may make the place untidy.
- Loud, talkative, and overbearing. They present as larger-than-life characters who like to dominate the conversation and are poor listeners. They have a lot of potential but do not use it in an effective way.
- Highly successful, they give the appearance of having all aspects of life under control. Successful in work, they are financially well-off, with high-end possessions and good relationships with family and friends. They are also able to take time off for fun.
- Very involved with the church, they see the world through a religious filter. They find it difficult to understand how others cannot see the benefits of a life devoted to religion as it brings so much to their life.
- Very focused on being a mother, they see motherhood as the central role in their life. Their children are the center of their world and everything revolves around this.

(PS) "I would rather be surrounded by smart people than have a huge budget. Smart people will get you there faster." *Former McKinsey associate*

Why?

- Why do some cultures read from left to right, some from right to left, and some from top to bottom?

- Why does today's western society seem to value extroversion over introversion?
- Why does some people's hair go frizzy in the rain and some people's doesn't?
- Why do we use the phrase, "It's the best thing since sliced bread"?
- Why is it that food we like isn't usually good for us?

> **(CR)** "You can't depend on your eyes when your imagination is out of focus." *Mark Twain, author*

- If black is supposed to absorb heat and white reflect it, why are people with very white skin native to cold countries?
- Why are you using this book?
- Why do fashions change?
- Why are there so many belief systems?
- Why do people like to buy the same clothes that famous people wear?

> **(CO)** "His conversation does not show the minute hand; but he strikes the hour very correctly." *Samuel Johnson, author*

Words of One Syllable

To get a simple message across it's said that you need to talk in words of one syllable. This, however, is harder than it sounds. How do you say, for example, "yesterday," "uncle," or "Saturday"? Have a conversation using the topics below, where everyone has to speak in words of one syllable.

- What did you do yesterday?
- What are your plans for the weekend?
- Tell us about a summer vacation you had when you were a child.
- What jobs did your parents do when they first started working?
- Describe one of your grandparents' houses.

(TD) "No matter where you go or what you do, you live your entire life within the confines of your head." *Terry Josephson, businessman*

- What is your favorite type of animal?
- What do you think will be different in your life in a year's time?
- Which teacher do you most remember from your school days and why?
- If you had to choose a favorite superhero, who would it be?
- Tell us about the last book you read.

(CR) "The hardest thing about reality is returning to it after an hour inside your child's mind." *Robert Brault, author*

Work

- The average tea room at work is boring! This is what tea rooms should be like ...
- What would happen if, one day a month, the chief exec had to work as the office cleaner?

- It's a good idea to let people take as many holidays as they like, because ...
- What could be a completely new way of job sharing?
- Surely it's possible to have a Bring Your Mom or Dad to Work Day?

(PS) "If the only tool you have is a hammer, you tend to see every problem as a nail." *Abraham Maslow, psychologist*

- If you were interviewing someone for a job and they asked to see your credentials to check you were qualified, what would you do?
- Devise a different kind of team building day that would really build a team.
- To motivate staff, the manager should start every day with ...
- Sleep specialists say that employees work better and are more efficient if they have a forty-minute power nap at three o'clock in the afternoon. From a practical point of view, how would this work?
- When companies do well, instead of giving their staff a financial bonus, employees should receive ...

(TD) "You and I are not what we eat; we are what we think." *Walter Anderson, painter*

Writing

- Give a quick synopsis of the rest of the story that starts with, "Once upon a time there was a princess who wanted to be a truck driver."

- Give the first line of a story that ends with, ". . . and so he always went to psychotherapy sessions with his teddy bear."
- Why do writers get writer's block if they are passionate about writing?
- Do you think that William Shakespeare, a poorly educated and untraveled lower class person with little knowledge of the world, actually wrote his plays?
- With regard to detective novels, what kind of personality is the least likely to be a successful detective?

(PS) "Take time to deliberate, but when the time for action has arrived, stop thinking and go in." *Napoleon Bonaparte, military commander*

- If Stephen King, author of contemporary horror and suspense novels, had written a book with Barbara Cartland, author of tame fictional romantic novels, what would the book have been like?
- You have been asked to write a weekly column in your local newspaper about, "Quirky people and events in our community." What's the first thing that springs to mind you could write about?
- You notice an autobiographical book in the bookshop titled, *How I Got Rich Even Though I'm Not Intelligent.* Which celebrity might have written it, and what would their message be?
- Would people follow a blog titled, "Boring things that happened today"?
- Are nonfiction books concerning communicating with aliens actually fact or fiction?

(CR) "Do not covet your ideas. Give away everything you know, and more will come back to you." *Paul Arden, author*

You

- Describe yourself in twenty words or less.
- Describe a more extreme version of yourself in twenty words or less.
- Imagine you had had your memory wiped and didn't know who you were. If you were to go into your house on your own and look round, what do you think you could work out about who you are and the life you've created for yourself?
- If you wanted to "sell" your life on an auction site so that someone could slot into your job, home, hobbies, family, etc. and live as you do, what would be the main selling points?
- Be honest, what do you think when you look in the mirror?

(TD) "Nothing is more conducive to peace of mind than not having any opinion at all." *G. C. Lichtenberg, scientist*

- Who do you know who most looks like you? Which features are similar?
- Who do you know who most thinks like you? What ways of thinking do you have in common?
- Are you nosy?
- What is your most unique aspect?
- What is the most regular, dominant thought you have?

(PS) "Never tell people *how* to do things. Tell them *what* to do and they will surprise you with their ingenuity." *George S. Patton, military commander*

You Can Do Anything!

What would you do, and what would happen, if you had no fear about:

- Going on a huge adventure.
- Looking stupid.
- Your career.
- Your relationship.
- Moving to live somewhere else.

> **(CR)** "If anybody laughs at your idea, view it as a sign of potential success!" *Jim Rogers, investor*

- Money.
- Your health.
- Your abilities.
- What other people thought of you.
- Being too old to . . .

(PS) "The best way to resolve any problem in the human world is for all sides to sit down and talk." *Dalai Lama*

You Walk into a Room And . . .

- . . . are invited to spend an hour in one of the areas in the room. In one area is a comfortable chair and a selection of magazines; in another is a table, chair, paper, pens, pencils, paintbrushes, and paint; and in the other is a comfortable chair, TV, remote, and TV programme guide. Which is the most appealing?

- ...there is someone waiting to see you, someone you were at school with when you were ten years old who wants to meet up with you. Who would it be?
- ...there are three mirrors. One shows you as you are now; one shows you as you used to be when you were younger; and one shows you as who you would like to be. Is there much difference in what the mirrors show?
- ...there is a gift-wrapped box on a table. What would you like to find in the box?
- ...there are two doors leading out of the room, one marked, "The safe, easy route" and one marked, "The risky route." Which door would you choose?

(CR) "I paint objects as I think them, not as I see them." *Pablo Picasso, painter*

- ...there are three chairs, each with a phone and piece of paper on it. The paper tells you who is on the other end of the phone. You are to have a conversation with one of the people. Who would you choose: a comedian; a personal motivation coach; or someone wanting advice on a topic you are skilled at?
- ...there are several people dressed as Roman gladiators. One of them approaches you and says "We've been waiting for you." What could be going on?
- ...there is a cocktail party in full swing. You don't know anyone but want to give the air of being confident when you approach people. How would you do it?
- ...it's an old-fashioned living room at evening time and you are told that there is a ghost in the room. You are asked to spend an hour in the room on your own to see if anything unusual happens. Would you do it?
- ...it's a time machine. The date is set to two years in the future. Would you go?

(CO) "A lot of good arguments are spoiled by some fool who knows what he is talking about." *Miguel de Unamuno, novelist*

Your Call!

Fill in the blanks to make your own customized conversation starters!

- If the world were to end tomorrow, would you_____?
- If you were in a place where no one knew you, would you like to _____?
- I bet that when you were a child you _____.
- What on earth made you decide to _____?
- When you were at school I imagine you got told off for _____.

(CR) "Things are only impossible until they're not." *Jean-Luc Picard, Star Trek captain*

- How often have you considered _____?
- If I gave you a million dollars, would you _____?
- Would you ever go for an evening out with _____?
- If your life depended on it, could you _____?
- If you were stranded on a desert island, would you _____?

(CO) "Are you really listening, or are you just waiting for your turn to speak?" *John Milton Fogg, author*

Your Favorites & Your Starters

Here you can make a note of any of your favorite starters and compile a list of your own questions and conversation starters.